I highly recommend this eye-opening study on the life and leadership of King David. This is no storybook hero. Dr. Rutland reveals the real King David to be a complicated, flawed but wonderfully anointed leader in a treacherous world.

—JENTEZEN FRANKLIN
SENIOR PASTOR, FREE CHAPEL
NEW YORK TIMES BEST-SELLING AUTHOR

In our troubled generation we need a fresh understanding of King David. We do not need so much the bedtime story David. We need David raw, David complex, David a man of his times. Even more, we need David the fully human man of God. Dr. Mark Rutland gives us this and more in his invaluable study of the great king.

—STEPHEN MANSFIELD, PhD
NEW YORK TIMES BEST-SELLING AUTHOR

DAVID
THE
GREAT

MARK RUTLAND

CHARISMA
HOUSE

Most CHARISMA HOUSE BOOK GROUP products are available at special quantity discounts for bulk purchase for sales promotions, premiums, fund-raising, and educational needs. For details, write Charisma House Book Group, 600 Rinehart Road, Lake Mary, Florida 32746, or telephone (407) 333-0600.

DAVID THE GREAT by Mark Rutland
Published by Charisma House
Charisma Media/Charisma House Book Group
600 Rinehart Road
Lake Mary, Florida 32746
www.charismahouse.com

Unless otherwise noted, all Scripture quotations are taken from the Holy Bible, New Living Translation, copyright © 1996, 2004, 2007. Used by permission of Tyndale House Publishers, Inc., Wheaton, IL 60189. All rights reserved.

Scripture quotations marked ESV are from the Holy Bible, English Standard Version. Copyright © 2001 by Crossway Bibles, a division of Good News Publishers. Used by permission.

Scripture quotations marked KJV are from the King James Version of the Bible.

Scripture quotations marked NKJV are taken from the New King James Version®. Copyright © 1982 by Thomas Nelson. Used by permission. All rights reserved.

Cover design by Justin Evans

Visit the author's website at www.globalservants.org.

Library of Congress Cataloging-in-Publication Data:
An application to register this book for cataloging has been submitted
to the Library of Congress.
International Standard Book Number: 978-1-62999-526-7
E-book ISBN: 978-1-62999-527-4

18 19 20 21 22 — 9 8 7 6 5 4 3 2
Printed in the United States of America

If I forget thee, O Jerusalem, let my right
hand forget its cunning.

———

CONTENTS

Part III—Evening | 139

A LETTER TO THE READER

Dear Reader,

For this, my fifteenth book, I chose an informal style, more of a conversational tone. I hope you will feel that I am talking to you person-to-person, over coffee perhaps, or rather in an intimate lecture hall. I strove in this book, as in nothing I have written before, to maintain the illusion that I am your jovial old professor, trying desperately to make the Bible and this particular king called David come alive for you, even if I must go against the rules of grammar to do it. Indeed that is exactly how this book began. I taught the life and times of King David multiple times at two wonderful universities where I served as president. Those lectures proved to be the most popular I ever gave. I was gratified beyond measure to see millennials, and their professors for that matter, pack rooms both grand and small to hear the truth about the Lion of the Tribe of Judah.

I set out to shred the Sunday-school, felt-board David and show them the real man, the David of the Bible. I wanted them to learn life lessons from the grit and grime of David's life—his real life, not the Americanized, little Christian shepherd boy with his toy slingshot. I strove to tell them the truth, and they and I discovered together that truth is sometimes ugly and complex and messy. We also discovered that truth is worth the mess. I wanted them to listen, of course, but more than that, I wanted them hear, which is a different thing. Frankly, I did not know if they would tolerate the darkness in order to find the light. I was surprised and delighted that, far from being disgusted by the real King David, they couldn't get enough. They wanted to know David and to hear about his heart for God and, yes, why he sinned as he did. They wanted to understand David. I was afraid that if I made them see his failures, they would dismiss him as that—a failure. Far from it. They said, "Now this, this ancient king, this is a man we can listen to. This is a voice for our turbulent times." I feared they would be repelled by the contradictions in David's life. They impressed me deeply with their willingness, nay, eagerness to get down in the muck and dive for pearls.

In order to keep them engaged in the struggle, I took a storyteller's license with grammar. When I felt the need, I said, "At this point David's rides into town" rather than "rode" into town. It worked. Over the years, I have been asked by literally hundreds of students to do what I at last have done…write this very book.

I have chosen, therefore, to maintain a fluidity in tense, floating whimsically and quite ungrammatically between present and past tense, just as one might do telling a story rather than writing a textbook. This somewhat quirky violation of everything I learned in my Strunk style manual in college may be jarring to purists. This is not about grammar. This is about the real Lion King. Try to relax. At the same time, you'd best brace yourself. As we used to say in Texas, this is gonna get rowdy.

—MARK RUTLAND

INTRODUCTION

———

IN ALL OF history, very few people have been afforded the title "Great." Mother Russia had Catherine, England had Alfred, Greece had Alexander, and Persia had Cyrus, but the United States has never used the title at all, not even once. There is no "Lincoln the Great" or "Patton the Great." It is that rarest of all historical titles, lusted after and fought for, yet seldom given to the kings of the earth.

The title "Great" is reserved in history for those people who—though perhaps not great in the sense of morality—are simply larger than life, huge personalities on the stage of human history.

In the bitterest of historical ironies, the only monarch in Israel's history to be called "Great" was Herod, a consummate psychopath, whose reign was a veritable bloodbath, not of glorious conquest but of heinous murder. Herod the Great killed so many of his own family that the emperor Augustus joked that it was better to be Herod's pig than his son.[1]

Yet Herod's "greatness," such as it was, derived from architecture, not glory in battle. He was a great builder of structures, including the famed temple in Jerusalem, but he was also a horrendous destroyer of lives. Nevertheless, he is to this day called Herod the Great.

The only king of Israel who merited the honor of being called the Great was not the maniacal Herod, to be sure, but a complex and controversial man who predated Herod by a thousand years, David of Bethlehem.

Even those dismissive of the Bible cannot deny that David is among the most famous names in world literature. Were David nothing but a myth, his story would still be the stuff of the greatest of legends. Giant slayer, warrior chieftain, outlaw, mercenary, lover, poet, musician, and sometime prophet, David is great by any measure.

Sculpted, painted, debated, denounced, and denied, David is the greatest of all Israel's rulers. Among the kings of his own or any other age, hardly a man like David exists. He is considered the true father of his nation, though Saul was its first king. One cannot fully understand the history of Israel, nor have a true sense of the Bible as a whole story, without David.

Still, some might be hesitant to utter the phrase "David the Great," and understandably so. For every Goliath in the story of David, there is a Bathsheba around the corner. For every soul to whom he showed compassion, there were a hundred he was personally responsible for slaughtering. He had many wives, yet his palace was also filled with concubines. He had a different woman for every night of the week.

During one lengthy period David was an outlaw who ran what can only be called a protection racket. Later he was a mercenary raider who sold his skills to his people's adversaries. He was dreaded by his enemies not only for killing them in great numbers but, as they saw it, also for sometimes mutilating and desecrating the bodies of the fallen for little more than a bizarre bridal dowry. His own father-in-law hated him. At least one of his wives despised and betrayed him. One of his sons led a revolution against him and would have executed him had not more loyal souls intervened. David caused a devastating plague and, like a Mafia don, ordered the execution of his enemies while on his deathbed.

Yet he was also a Spirit-sensitive poet whose words have comforted millions worldwide in two major religions for three thousand years. He was a musician whose songs could soothe a demon-haunted soul. He was a political leader strong enough to forge a single nation out of disparate tribes that had been ripped apart for years by civil war and internecine prejudice. Not least of all, David was a man of passionate loyalty, great faith, and national vision. The name of this ancient Jewish king is known where the Bible is not even read or believed.

We must remember though that David was not a twenty-first-century Christian. If we try to dress him in a suit and tie and apply our standards of morality to his life, it simply won't work.

Jesus's teachings on loving your enemies? After David. Paul's writings on marriage, specifically monogamy? After David. Peter's call to not repay evil with evil? You get the point.

The story of the real David, the one I want to introduce you to, the one the Bible describes, could only be found in the adult graphic novel section of your comic book store. There would be no bright colors, capes, or pretty girls being rescued. That's not the Bible's David. The real David steals the pretty girls from their husbands. The real David makes a mess of his family. The real David breaks the laws of both God and man. We need to "de-comic-book" David and tell the real story.

The reality is that while David was no saint, neither was he a monster. He was a complex man, perhaps one of the most complicated and conflicted leaders of all time. He was a multi-faceted genius whose abilities in seemingly mutually exclusive genres are unparalleled. He could make war and write soul-piercing poetry with equal facility. We may well be shocked by his sins, but we are also inspired by his victories and moved by his intimacy with the God of Abraham. There is much, ever so much, to learn from his life.

Some years ago, I sat writing at a picnic table in Tiberias, Israel. With my manuscript stacked neatly on the table, I was writing at such a furious pace that at first I did not notice the middle-aged woman watching me. When I looked up, she asked if I was an American. When I said yes, she asked what I was writing about.

"King David," I answered.

"King David?"

"Yes, you know, from the Bible."

"Why?" she asked with disdain. "Why in the world would you write about that bloody man?"

Obviously, she cherished no notion of him as David the Great, and I knew it was useless to try to explain my lifelong fascination with an ancient king who had ruled so long ago in her land. I asked myself: How great a man is he whose controversy outlives him by millennia? How great is a man who can inspire equal parts of vitriol, admiration, and curiosity for three thousand years?

So here he is: David, King of Israel, "that bloody man" who was also a man after God's own heart.

PROLOGUE

In those days Israel had no king, so the people
did whatever seemed right in their own eyes.

—JUDGES 21:25

Look no further than the final verse in the book of Judges to describe the era in which David arose: "The people did whatever seemed right in their own eyes."

Although David is the lead character in the story of the birth of the nation of Israel, the second character is the time in which he lived. David lived in an era far different from ours, so different, in fact, that truly understanding what that period was like defies the most fertile imagination.

The genealogy in Matthew 1 helps put David's moment in history into perspective. "Salmon was the father of Boaz (whose mother was Rahab). Boaz was the father of Obed (whose mother was Ruth). Obed was the father of Jesse. Jesse was the father of King David" (vv. 5–6).

We are not sure who Salmon was, but he may have been one of the spies sent into Jericho by Joshua. Rahab was the pagan prostitute who helped the Hebrew spies before they invaded Jericho. Salmon and Rahab, sometime after the fall of Jericho, married and had a boy they named Boaz. Boaz became kinsman-redeemer for a Moabite Gentile named Ruth for whom the Book of Ruth is named. Boaz married Ruth, and they became the parents of Obed, who was the father of Jesse, who was the father of David.

David, then, was only three generations away from the Gentile Ruth and four generations from the harlot Rahab. This also meant that just five generations before David, the future king's great-great-great-grandfather was born into slavery. And his great-great-grandfather was born in the desert under a pillar of fire sometime after his parents were freed from Egypt. Today it's not unusual to see photos from family reunions that include five generations. That is how close King David was to his people's time as slaves in Egypt.

In fact, merely one generation before David, until Saul became king, no real nation of Israel existed. The land was certainly there, but there was no central government, no standing army, and no monarchy—only a loose confederation of agrarian tribes that knew little about warfare. These Hebrew tribes bickered and fought among themselves to the point of outright combat.

Throughout the land, there were also various pagan groups and tribes that surrounded, mingled with, and terrorized the Hebrew people. To the south were the Amalekites, a depraved people who were violent raiders. They were to Israel what Vikings were to England during the early medieval period. To the west, the Philistines, while more sophisticated governmentally, were still barbaric and cruel. They had one military invention that gave them an advantage over the Hebrews: iron. The Hebrew people had only bronze, but the Philistines fought with iron. Imagine an ancient game of Rock, Paper, Scissors but with only iron and bronze. Iron *always* beats bronze. The metal was so important that the Philistines forbade any Hebrew from owning iron or an iron forge.

Until the time of Saul, just before David, the Hebrews were still in the Bronze Age, with no organized government, no constitution or bylaws, and no king. They were surrounded by barbaric enemies, who constantly raided and plundered. It was the wild, wild west.

Judges 19 records an absolutely horrendous story that reveals exactly how spiritually bankrupt and governmentally primitive the tribes of Israel were at the time of Ruth, just before Saul became king. A Levite traveler and his concubine came late to a town where they knew no one. An old man offered them refuge so they wouldn't have to sleep on the street. When a group of men came to the old man's home demanding that he send out the Levite to them so that they could rape him, the Levite pushed his concubine out to them instead. The men raped her all night until she died. The next day, the Levite chopped up her body into twelve parts and sent them throughout the tribes of Israel as a call to action.

In a strange coincidence, this despicable event took place in Gibeah, the town where Saul was later anointed the first king of Israel.

Saul was certainly not Israel's greatest king, but he was the first. Based on the Judges 19 story, Saul clearly grew up in a time far from civilized. The Israelites had been begging the prophet and judge Samuel for a king of their own, and Saul, a massive human being said to be head and shoulders taller than the next tallest person, was the man God chose for the task.

Saul was a weak and carnal man, yet despite that he was an important person in the life of Israel. He took the loose and violent tribal confederation he inherited when he became king, with tribes scattered from Dan to Beersheba amid the surrounding pagan peoples, and created the seminal nation of Israel.

The land at that time was not a nation with clear boundaries. In North America, Canada is the nation to the north of the continent. Going south, the United States is next, then Mexico, and so forth. No part of Mexico exists in Canada, and none of the fifty United States are down near Guatemala. Yet that is what Israel was at the time of Saul and young David. A Hebrew family from the tribe of Benjamin might be living next to an Amalekite village. David himself, for example, was born in the town of Bethlehem within walking distance of Jebus, a major pagan stronghold that David the King would later transform into the new capital of Israel.

Clearly Saul inherited an untenable situation when he became King of Israel, and it is to his great credit that, to an extent, he brought national identity and monarchial order to a land where "people did whatever seemed right in their own eyes." Saul's downfall was spiritual and emotional weakness. He was in bondage to his emotions. He was up with God, then down with God. He was a great leader, then a bad leader, a bold leader, then a prideful leader. He was double-minded and unstable, and ultimately paranoid.

Finally, God had enough of Saul. Saul may have been king, but the Israelites were God's people, and He was determined to give them a new leader with a different heart. God sent the prophet Samuel to Saul to make this dreadful announcement.

In 1 Samuel 15, Samuel tells Saul, "Since you have rejected the LORD's command, he has rejected you from being the king of Israel.... The LORD has torn the kingdom of Israel from you today and has given it to someone else—one who is better than you" (vv. 26, 28).

Saul, the quintessential egotist, was stunned when Samuel told him the next king would be "one who is better than you." Imagine how that sounded to Saul. Not only "someone else," but someone "better than you."

Ultimately, Saul came to understand God's mind could not be changed. Instead, he pleaded with Samuel: "I know I have sinned. But please, at least honor me before the elders of my people and before Israel by coming back with me so that I may worship the LORD your God" (1 Sam. 15:30). In other words, Saul admitted in private that God had withdrawn His anointing from him and that he was no longer the king. Yet Saul begged to maintain the appearance of being king. He wanted to keep the power and the prestige—even if only for a short while.

Samuel agreed, and the withdrawal of Saul's anointing remained a secret between them.

Still, the road to kingship for "one who is better than" Saul had begun. For all spiritual purposes, that was the end of Saul's story. He was king for years afterward, but he was finished. Samuel left Gibeah for Bethlehem, the home of Naomi, Ruth, and Boaz. A man named Jesse (Ruth's grandson) lived in that village. Jesse had eight sons, the youngest of whom tended to his father's flock. The boy's name was David.

The two kings' lives would soon collide ferociously. One remained king in public, but was no longer king in reality. The other, while not yet a king in public, was a king in reality. One resided at a palace in Gibeah. The other lived in a sheep shed in Bethlehem. One was a mighty warrior, the king of a fledgling nation, while the other was a shepherd boy, both ridiculed and envied by his older brothers.

How would God bring these two kings together? And when He did, what would happen when a power-crazy, emotionally bankrupt, psychopathic, murderous king who wanted to retain his hold on the throne crossed paths with an innocent, guileless adolescent upon whom rested the hand of God?

PART I

MORNING

———

I F DAVID HAD written an autobiography, I believe he would have emphasized that being the choice of God isn't all it's cracked up to be. Any person seeking to live for God faces excruciatingly tough decisions. Living out that passion for God in such a violent era as David's is what makes his story so raw and so maddeningly complex.

It could be said that because of Saul's failures, God stripped David of his childhood. When most young boys are concerned with games, not national celebrity, David was being anointed king of Israel. At the age an average teenager today learns to drive, David cut off the head of a giant. During the years today's young adults attend college, start their careers, and plan their futures, David was an outlaw hiding in caves.

David's early life is gut checking. His life makes us rethink the whole question of what it means to be set apart by God for great things. Between David's anointing and his public coronation, decades of waiting, and bloodshed, and waiting, and running, and waiting, and deceiving, and waiting pass by. Years of waiting.

Being a man after God's own heart means living life open and submitted to God's will and timing. It means telling Him, "I'm Yours, and I will trust in You, no matter what." In David's case, "no matter what" meant no matter how many spears his father-in-law threw at him.

CHAPTER 1

A STRANGE BOY TO SAY THE LEAST

Based on 1 Samuel 16

WHEN DAVID FIRST appeared in the story that was to become his, he was a shepherd boy. His life was far from those of the romanticized shepherds of modern stories. In David's day, the shepherd in the family was the runt, the youngest, and often the most despised by his elders, who was made a shepherd because he was not capable of much else.

David had seven older brothers, grown men who were strong warriors. They endured their younger brother—barely. Jesse's seven older sons thought David was strange, to say the least, and a bragging little liar, to say the worst.

From his earliest days, David's life had a touch of the miraculous. Consider the fact that David was a master musician at a prodigious age. Prodigies are often hated by their less-talented elders. Then there were his accounts of supernatural victories in the wilderness. Imagine an evening meal in David's family home: He has returned with his sheep, cleaned up, and joined his older, larger brothers at the kitchen table. Challenged by their mother to be nicer to David, they fire off questions between bites.

"What did you do today, little brother?" one asks before immediately turning to his mother to make sure she noticed his "effort."

Guileless as the child he is, David answers without hesitation. "Today I killed a lion."

Imagine the ridicule, the mockery he must have endured. Perhaps Eliab, the eldest, led the verbal assault. "Killed a lion, did you? Wow! That must have been dangerous business. It's a miracle you weren't killed."

"Yes," agrees the naïve child. "It was a miracle. A great miracle."

"How did you kill the ferocious beast?"

David, oblivious to the sarcasm, answers, "I punched him."

Imagine the laughter. Gales of laughter.

David begins to realize he is being mocked, but he presses on. "Yes, he ran at the sheep, and I hit him with my fist."

"And he died? Just like that? Wow!"

By now, everyone is up to speed on the conversation. The brothers are laughing together, and Jesse and his wife are smiling awkwardly and shaking their heads.

"Yes, he died. Just like the bear."

"Oh, a bear too. A lion and a bear. What a warrior. What a mighty slayer of beasts is this sweet singer of songs."

After what feels like an eternity to David, his father, Jesse, raises his hand, and the laughter ceases. "OK, David. Are you saying you killed a lion?"

"And a bear," Abinadab adds. "Don't forget the bear, Father."

"And a bear?" Jesse asks. "A lion and a bear?"

"Yes," David responds quietly.

Jesse looks into the innocent eyes of his youngest and says, "The next time you kill a lion or a bear, why don't you cut off its head? Bring that head home and show it to your brothers. To all of us. No one calls anyone in this family a liar, and we're not calling you a liar, son, but next time, bring the head."

THE PROPHET ARRIVES

One day, the prophet Samuel arrived in town. This was a big deal, especially in a village like Bethlehem. No paparazzi follow him, but Samuel was the most famous religious leader of his day. Samuel walking into Bethlehem would be something like a rock star today suddenly appearing in a small town or Billy Graham showing up at a country church.

Since anointing Saul as the first king of Israel, Samuel had nearly retired and taken a back seat in the kingdom. His return to the scene, his arrival in Bethlehem, was something of a scary moment. There was serious apprehension. What did this mean? The Scriptures even say that the elders of the town were afraid upon seeing Samuel, and they hadn't even learned the reason he was there (1 Sam. 16:4). They would have been shocked to learn that the reason for Samuel's appearance was treason—anointing a new king when a perfectly healthy king sat on the throne.

Samuel doesn't waste any time upon entering Bethlehem. Samuel was hardly a folksy chap on his sunniest day. He is there on serious business. He tells the elders of the town, "Gather at Jesse's house for a sacrifice to the Lord."

"Jesse's house? What for?" Some of them might have been wondering if he had come to rebuke Jesse's youngest for blasphemy. Had the boy's bizarre stories of miracles offended the great prophet?

"I'm going there to anoint a new king," Samuel answers. The elders are shocked—probably horrified.

"Look, uh…listen, we don't want to argue with a prophet. Please don't strike us dead or anything, OK? We're with you, alright? But, well, we do have just one tiny, maybe important, maybe not, question: What about Saul?"

Without hesitation, Samuel responds bluntly, "What about him? I have nothing to do with Saul anymore. The next king is in Jesse's house."

That said, everyone gathers at Jesse's house. The torches are lit, the elders are assembled, there's a fearful mysteriousness in the room. Samuel goes straight to Jesse's oldest, strongest son, Eliab. He is a perfect specimen of a man. "He looks kingly,"

Samuel thinks to himself. "He's not Saul exactly, but he's impressive enough." Samuel holds out the oil, ready to anoint Eliab, when he feels a spiritual check.

"This isn't the one."

He looks to the next biggest one, Abinadab. Again, "This isn't the one." The same story with Shimea and all the other brothers present. "This isn't the one... This isn't the one... This isn't the one..."

After going through all seven brothers, Samuel's next words to Jesse prompt one of the funniest exchanges in the Bible: "Are you sure these are all your sons?"

"Am I sure these are all my sons?" Jesse asks in disgust. "What are you accusing me of? What's wrong with my boys here? What do you mean, are these all my sons?"

"Well, are they?"

Silence.

"Are they? I count seven sons. Is this right, Jesse?"

Jesse becomes quiet and looks away before answering. "There, well, there is another... out in the fields somewhere. The youngest. He is... well... What can I say?"

Samuel responds, "Let's see what God sees in him. Go find him now. We will not sit down or eat one bite until he is here."

When David eventually arrives and sees everyone staring at him, he must have been thinking to himself, "What did I do now?" Quietly he asks them, "Do you want to hear a song?"

He has absolutely no idea what's happening, but as the youngest he's used to being left out of the loop. Samuel walks over to this skinny child, smelling like sheep, with knees like a camel, a sunburned nose, tousled hair, and a banjo slung over his shoulder.

Perhaps Samuel himself argued with God. "Oh, Lord, no. Not this one, surely not this one."

Samuel listens for the only opinion that matters. The words come. "This is the one." Immediately, Samuel tilts the horn, pours oil on David, and anoints him as the next king of Israel.

His brothers' reactions must have been priceless. Surely not aloud, not so Samuel could hear it, but they must have chafed. All their anger and envy must have made that mysterious evening a bitter pill to swallow.

Then there were Bethlehem's village elders. They must have been afraid. They were present at this treasonous ceremony. If Saul found out about this, they knew he would kill them all and perhaps burn Bethlehem to the ground.

David has no more idea than the others of what has happened to him. Nobody explained anything to him. He just came in out of the field, and an old man poured oil on his head. He looked to his dad with an uncertain look on his face.

"You only have yourself to blame, son," Jesse says to him. "If you want to kill lions and bears with your bare hands, this is what happens."

LESSON FROM OLD DR. MARK

There will be moments in your life when God does something that resonates deeply with you. They ping on your sonar screen, and you just know that something big is going to happen. Then years go by, and nothing happens. The lost years don't erase God's mark on you though. The announcement was still made. The time has simply not yet come.

THE NEXT STEP: WAIT

Perhaps even stranger than this scene with an old man pouring oil over a boy is that when it's over...it's just over. Samuel goes back to his lonely prophet's retreat, and David returns to his sheep. Everything goes back to normal. Or so it seems.

Yet nothing is ever normal again. God has made His mark on David, and David's story was just beginning. However, it's important to remember that David's story was not the only story being written. Saul's story was not yet finished. Just because David was anointed didn't mean it was time for him to take the next step. Rather, it was time for the next step, but that next step was simply to wait.

God withdrew His anointing from Saul, who, in turn, fell into a demonic nightmare world. He was filled with rage and was guilt-ridden. The Bible puts it like this, a puzzling verse for many: "An evil spirit from the LORD troubled him" (1 Sam. 16:14, KJV).

Saul's troubled soul and his tortured mind were of his own making. God simply let Saul live with the torments he carved out for himself.

Soon, Saul was having horrible nightmares and not sleeping well at all. A kind-hearted minion in his camp says to the king, "Hey, I heard about a kid over in Bethlehem who can play and sing better than anyone in Israel. Why don't I go get this kid, and we'll see if he can sing you to sleep?"

Saul is willing to try anything at this point, so he summons David to his camp. Now what could David have been thinking at this point? Not too long before, the most famous spiritual leader in Israel poured oil over his head and said that David was God's choice to be the next king. Now the current king is sending for him? Did Saul know?

What's going to happen to David?

When young David arrives in the king's tent, Saul is tossing and turning and moaning behind a veil. All the oil lamps have been turned down, save for one flickering light. And the captain of the guard simply says to David, "Sit over there, and play and sing for the king. See if you can get him to sleep."

Here's young David, away from home and probably frightened. Secretly he knows he is supposed to be the next king, but he's told to play and sing for the current sleepless and tormented old king. It's a very odd and frightening moment in the young boy's life. Yet odd circumstances are nothing new for David.

David plays, and at last the king sleeps. In time, David is sent back to Bethlehem. Saul and his army head out for battle, and nothing else happens for David. It's over. He simply goes back to shepherding.

And that's exactly where God wanted him right then.

Leadership Focus: Promotion comes from the Lord.

Young people today spend way too much time trying to force their way into opportunities. In fact, nobody is really immune to this. Whether we're fresh out of college or twenty years into a profession, when we see even the hint of an opportunity, our initial instinct may be to push the door open ourselves.

We dare not promote ourselves to our next job. We cannot force others to see what only we can see, or think we see, in ourselves and kick-start our destiny into a higher gear. Promotion doesn't come from us or even from others. Promotion comes from the Lord, and the Lord only.

You are where you are right now because where you are is where God wants to use you right now. Maybe you've been told you're going to be the next king. Are you king now? David wasn't. David did his job there, right where he was. He was a shepherd, and he did it well. He was gifted in music, and he used it well. When he was given an opportunity to sing and play for—of all people—his demon-possessed predecessor, he did it well.

Wait on the Lord for your next opportunity. When that opportunity comes, don't get caught in the snare of assigning too much significance to it. After David sang Saul to sleep, he didn't snoop around and start planning a hostile takeover. He didn't say to himself, "God has finally brought me to my destiny. It's time to start my kingdom!" He did what he was brought there to do and then went home to his sheep.

David had an opportunity to serve the king, and he did it well. That is all God wanted from him at the time. His moment to become the ruling king had not yet arrived.

Follow David's lead. Learn to wait on the Lord. Trust in His timing. Let God guide you to Saul's camp. Let God work on Saul. Let God work on you. Let God work on Samuel. Eventually, all these lines intersect at just the right moment. At God's moment.

God is in control of your life, and He is working at different places and at different times to get you where you need to be at just the right time.

Wait on the Lord. Let God promote you in His own way and in His own time. Arriving at the right place is good, of course. Arriving there at the right time is even better.

CHAPTER 2

THE SHADOW KING

Based on 1 Samuel 17

On a battlefield in the valley of Elah, a teenage David stood before the entire Israeli army—seasoned veterans twice his age, carrying swords and shields with the bloodstains of war upon them—and shouted and called them out. "Is there not a cause? Are you going to allow this behemoth to insult our God like this? Do you not believe that God will give you victory over this blasphemous brute?"

Though still an adolescent, with less experience in battle than the donkeys carrying the army's tents, young David was courageous and mature in faith. Long before he became a king, prior to living as a refugee and outlaw, David could recognize who were his real enemies and who were not, who needed to be put in their place and who were to still be respected, who he needed to take out of the picture and who needed to be left in God's hands.

Every leader is going to acquire enemies. It's part of the package that comes with a title. A king of Israel has many enemies. A wise leader recognizes that some apparent enemies are not true enemies, and some who seem to be friends are lethal.

Being placed on a path toward kingship at such a young age gave David ample opportunity to learn about enemies. Perhaps David's greatest leadership gift in his youth was in knowing which enemies were his to deal with and which were to be dealt with by the living God.

LOYALTY TO THE KING

Scripture gives no clear indication that Saul and David met face-to-face during those evenings in the tent when David sang to the restless king. That may seem strange, but we would be ill-advised to assume that Saul and David built some kind of father-and-son relationship. Perhaps it happened, but more likely it didn't. Saul was, after all, a king and David a visiting minstrel.

The king's tent was not a pup tent like that of a Boy Scout. Rather, Saul's tent would've been quite large, perhaps with a veil hanging down that separated his sleeping area from the rest of the tent. When David was brought in with his lyre, Saul was probably already in bed, tossing and turning, perhaps struggling with his demons. The king's pitiable groaning must have unnerved a sheltered boy from a rural village.

David was likely told to sit across the room on pillows laid out for him and to sing a few songs until the king drifted into a peaceful night's sleep. Then David was excused to go back to the baggage tent where he slept. That went on for an undetermined amount of time before Saul felt he was better and ready to go on a military campaign. Thus, the two kings' paths diverged once again.

We do not know if the two kings ever met face-to-face during that time. We do know that David, the young shadow king, did not begin a mutiny during these long nights when King Saul was perhaps at his most vulnerable. David did not spread the rumor around camp that Saul had lost his anointing from God. He did not let on that he, a boy who killed lions and bears with his hands, had been told by the prophet Samuel himself that he was to be the next king.

Instead, David was loyal to Saul. He honored him. He pitied him and sought to comfort him as much as he could with his God-given musical abilities. At this early point in their story, David did not know all the reasons God had taken Saul's anointing away or what Saul had done to bring upon himself such demonic torture. That was between God and Saul.

Knowing he was God's chosen next king, David remained loyal to King Saul, an unworthy man.

Even in later years, when it would be safe to say that Saul had become David's sworn enemy, David remained loyal to his king. David refused to kill the man who was trying to kill him. On two occasions, David could have killed Saul and seized the throne that was rightfully his, but he wouldn't do it.

This strange sense of loyalty to the man trying to kill him makes David seem like a fool to many in the modern world. Saul hated David, but David loved Saul. Saul threw a javelin to kill David, but David later stood over Saul while he slept and did him no harm. Saul certainly considered David his enemy, but David considered Saul his king.

Saul was David's king—an unworthy king, but his king nevertheless. If David had lifted his hand against Saul, whether in the tent as a boy or on the battlefield as a young man, instead of becoming the greatest king of Israel, he would have been replaced just as quickly as Saul was.

David sinned. Oh, did he ever sin. His were not puny sins, but the strength of David's character—what made him David the Great—was rooted in his indisputable conviction of two things: loyalty to the people of God and loyalty to the God of the people. As a man of God, David, until Saul's dying day, viewed the Israelite king as *his* king. During all his years on the run, David refused to stretch out a violent hand against the man God had once anointed king. In David's eyes, God had appointed Saul as king, and God must be the one to remove him as king.

At a surprisingly young age, David had the amazing wisdom not to touch Saul—not in the tent that first night their paths crossed, and not on the battlefield years later. Saul made David his enemy. David refused to make Saul his. The young, anointed king-to-be would indeed have plenty of enemies throughout his life, none larger than the man called Goliath.

LESSON FROM OLD DR. MARK

You would do better to be loyal to an unworthy person than to lift up your hand against the one whom God has put in place. If a pastor, or boss, or other leader is wrong or wicked, let God deal with it. Let God expose the sin. Let God remove that person. Remain faithful or simply leave. You always have the right to leave. You don't have to sit there and let somebody put a javelin in your throat. You just don't have the right to pull the javelin out of the wall and throw it back.

FACING THE GIANT

The story of David and Goliath has been so "Bible storyized" that it's hard to truly grasp it today. There is so much more to the story than the children's Bible version of a fearless, handsome boy who, despite being too small to wear the king's armor, slays a giant with only a rock. Not that the popular stories are wrong; they're just vastly incomplete.

David was still an adolescent at the time of the battle that turned him into a living legend. Too young to serve in Saul's army like his brothers Eliab, Abinadab, and Shimea, the skinny teenage boy remained a shepherd and the errand boy of his father, Jesse.

Nevertheless, the warrior was already inside the boy, and he looked forward to those times when his father would send him to Saul's camp to bring a message or some food to his brothers. On one particular trip to the army, David found the Philistines and Israelites camped on opposite hills across the valley of Elah. David listened in shock as a Philistine champion strode boldly into full view and challenged the Israelites to send out a champion of their own for a winner-take-all, man-to-man personal combat.

This was the ancient custom. The concept was that two champions would fight and the loser's army would lay down their arms and surrender without anyone else having to die. Of course, that rarely happened, for no army wants to go down without a fight. Typically, the two-man battle merely served as entertainment, a warm-up if you will, before the real battle.

When the young shepherd arrived at the battlefield with bread and cheese for his brothers and their captain, he set eyes for the first time on the Philistine giant, Goliath, who had been taunting the Israelites for forty days.

When describing Goliath, the Bible doesn't use the word *giant* frivolously. The man was more than nine feet tall. In fact, he belonged to a family of giants, with four brothers who were all gargantuan brutes. They were not monsters, just especially large humans, particularly when compared to David, who was still waiting for his muscles to develop.

David, standing there with the groceries, looks up and down the line of battle-hardened soldiers, with their armor and their spears and their swords—a fierce bunch to be sure. "So which one of you is gonna go kill this guy? This should be awesome. Looks like I arrived at just the right time."

"Uh, it's kinda my lunchtime," one of the soldiers says.

"My ankle is hurting."

"I would, but I fought the last champion, and I don't want to be typecast as 'that guy.'"

"I don't want to die today."

At least one of them was honest.

David can't believe what he's hearing. These are the best soldiers Israel has to offer? His own brothers are among them. Do they not know that they fight for the Lord's army?

"Well, what if I fought him?" David asks. "What do I get if I kill this foreigner?"

Probably assuming the kid was joking, the soldiers humor him and tell him about the prizes King Saul has offered to anyone who defeats the Philistine giant. He'd be given treasure, be made a general in the army, and get to marry Saul's daughter. In addition, his entire family would never again have to pay taxes.

The adolescent's eyes were bigger than his biceps. "OK, then. Let's do this! If you won't stand against this heathen who dares to defy the army of the living God, then I will."

At this point, David's oldest brother, Eliab, recognizes his youngest brother's voice and comes storming toward him. "What are you doing over here, you little twerp? Shouldn't you be back home with your sheep and imaginary lions? I know your wicked heart, little brother!"

Just then, across the way, the Philistine giant roars once again: "I defy the armies of Israel this day; give me a man, that we may fight together" (1 Sam. 17:10, KJV).

David can't take this any longer. How can God's army, led by God's king, let this enemy humiliate them like this? Though he is about a foot shorter than all the soldiers around him, David lifts up his chin as high as it can go and shouts to all, "Is there not a cause? Are you going to allow this creature to insult our God like this? Do you not believe that God would give you victory over this blasphemous pagan?"

Eliab is fuming now. He's just been called out by his insolent little brother but is at a loss for what to say. David turns to his big brother and this time speaks only to him.

With the confidence that can come only from someone who has literally wrestled with a bear and won, he says, "You know what, brother? You're right. All these years you've been right. I didn't kill that lion. Or the bear...God did. He just used me to do it. If none of you are going to stand up to this pagan, who is ridiculing our people and our God, then in God's name, I will. Just like the lion and the bear, God will take him down too. And I'm going to let Him use me to do it."

LESSON FROM OLD DR. MARK

Warning: The person who simply does what's right in innocence of heart will look manipulative, scheming, showy, and self-centered to those who are cynical. Yet this person is not necessarily the arrogant, egotistical jerk others may claim him to be. He has simply separated himself from their sinful worldview, and he has vision others do not have.

There was nothing for David's brothers to say at this point. David was not going to be talked out of this. He left his father's house with the mission of feeding his brothers and their colleagues, but now his mission is to stand up for Israel and its Lord. He could do this because he had courage that was born of the gift of faith. He simply had a calm, quiet confidence that God was going to do this. "God helped me kill the lion. God helped me kill the bear. God will kill this Philistine giant. I don't know how. All I know, all I have is the weapon of a shepherd. I do not have a sword. What I have is a sling. It will be enough. I will collect some rocks out of the stream and listen for God's leading."

While every other soldier in Israel's army sees only the size of the giant, David sees the size of the God of Israel. David approaches the giant and actually begins to mock him. The kid who probably weighs a buck twenty soaking wet is mocking the nine-foot giant! Is he insane? Not in the least. Even as a teenager, David was giving us a hint of the genius military strategy he would use time and again to win battles and expand the kingdom.

Goliath has his own personal armor bearer whose job is to just walk alongside him and carry his gigantic shield. As long as Goliath was behind that shield, David's rocks will simply bounce off the mobile iron wall and fall harmlessly to the ground. Yet if David could irritate that arrogant Philistine champion enough to get him to charge ahead of his armor bearer...

David yells up at the giant, "You come to me with sword, spear, and javelin, but I come to you in the name of the LORD.... Today the LORD will conquer you, and I will kill you and..." (1 Sam. 17:45–46).

David stops himself mid threat, perhaps he smiles, and looks over toward his brothers.

In between his uproarious laughs, Goliath speaks up. "You'll kill me and what, little boy?"

When David finally grabs the attention of Eliab's eyes, he nods at him and turns back to the Philistine. "I'll cut off your head."

David's plan works just as he hoped. At this absolutely ludicrous threat, the laughing giant comes out from behind his armor bearer and charges at David, who calmly fits the first stone into his sling, twirls it over his head as he has done thousands of times, and releases it, smacking Goliath right between the eyes. Immediately, the giant falls facedown in the mud. Is he dead? David isn't sure. He soon will be. The wiry king-to-be grabs Goliath's sword—how heavy must an iron sword of someone nine feet tall be?—makes sure his brothers are watching, and cuts off the giant's head.

Remember, the Israelites were still living in the Bronze Age at this time. The Philistines had the only iron weapons and tools in the land, and they forbade the Israelites from ever owning anything iron, so as to always have the upper hand in a battle. When David picked up Goliath's iron sword and decapitated the giant with it, it was a powerful political statement to the Philistines: If you won't let us forge weapons, we'll take yours and kill you with them.

In one afternoon, David took off the head of a giant and gained the admiration of a nation. The fateful collision of two kings, David and Saul, was now inevitable.

Leadership Focus: Choose your enemies wisely.

How many times did your mother tell you, "Choose your friends wisely"? First day of kindergarten, middle school, high school, college? She wasn't wrong. Please don't tell her I said she was wrong. Of course we should choose our friends wisely.

More important than choosing our friends wisely though is choosing our enemies wisely. Whom will you oppose, and to whom will you be loyal? Whom will you serve, perhaps even when you vehemently disagree with them or have lost respect for them?

With whom will you stand toe to toe and say, "No. Not this. Not now. Not you. This cannot stand"?

Those God has placed over you—your boss, pastor, teacher—even if they try pinning you to the wall with a javelin, they are not your enemy. Flee if you must as David did, but do not trade punches. God put them in their position; let God take them down. Don't you think He's capable of doing so?

When the Scriptures tell us to submit to governing authorities (Rom. 13:1), no added caveat says, "Submit to governing authorities unless they oppose your views—then just let them have it." We are to submit to the authorities God has placed over us, period. Sometimes this will include people we have been too quick to label as our enemies.

Don't risk making an enemy of God or an enemy of the things of God. Drop the javelin, the hammer, the verbal punches—true though they may be—and remain a steadfast, loyal soldier, the way David chose to serve King Saul.

On the other hand, do not fear to declare yourself in enmity with satanic forces in high places. If you drape yourself in faith and use the weapons of God, you cannot lose. Your opposition to the satanic forces, along with your steadfast loyalty to non-enemies, may well be the refining fire of your character.

CHAPTER 3

THE NEW HEBREW IDOL

Based on 1 Samuel 18–20

W HEN DAVID TURNED and tossed Goliath's head at his brothers' feet, the remaining Philistines, all two to three feet shorter than their champion, ran for their lives back in the direction of Gath. With newfound confidence and inspiration from the shepherd boy, the Hebrew army charged after the Philistines and slaughtered them. The Bible says the bodies "were strewn all along the road from Shaaraim, as far as Gath and Ekron" (1 Sam. 17:52).

When the soldiers returned home, it wasn't King Saul to whom they raised a toast and whose stories they celebrated—it was David. The young shepherd became an overnight celebrity. Everyone was talking about him. He was the new Hebrew hero. "Saul has killed his thousands, and David his ten thousands!" (1 Sam. 18:7) became the pop song of the day.

Yet just as quickly as David had become the most famous person in the land, he also made the top ten most wanted list: King Saul's list.

LESSON FROM OLD DR. MARK

Someday, you may be a senior executive in a business or organization, and you will have an employee who is knocking out deals and rising up the ranks. He's the new "it" guy in the field and is being treated like a messiah. Yes, killing him would be a creative way to handle it, but I wouldn't recommend following Saul's approach. Instead, there's another way: Let him win. Put garlands around his neck to congratulate him, and take the credit for hiring him. If you live in an egotistical emotional shell that is threatened by the successes of your own staff, you're going to wind up destroying your own house—just as Saul did.

Remember that at this time there was no clear line of succession in Israel's monarchy because Saul was the first king. He wasn't born to the throne. He was plowing the fields one day when a strange man carrying a horn of oil anointed him as Israel's first king. Years later, he had absolutely no idea how the next king would come to power.

Would it be his son Jonathan? Or had God anointed the new king already? Had Saul unknowingly promised his daughter to the "one who is better than him" and given his successor direct access to his kingdom?

THE MOST FAMOUS WARRIOR

We have the benefit of reading these stories three thousand years after the fact. No one in Israel knew what we know. Saul was king, yet he lost the anointing. What exactly does that mean? David was the anointed king, yet he was not king. In fact, did he clearly know he was the next king? Remember, he came in from the fields one day and an old guy poured oil over him. Did anyone tell him what just happened? Surely the elders and his brothers who were in his house that day were too terrified to say anything to anyone for fear of Saul taking their lives.

And what about Saul? He was no longer the most famous warrior in Israel. Instead, it was a boy half his size who was too young to even serve in the army. Yet everyone was talking about David, even the soldiers back in the barracks: "Did you see that kid who cut off the giant's head? I don't care how young he is. I could follow him."

Saul heard the murmuring around camp. He probably even offered a toast or two in David's honor, to appear as though he loved the boy just as much as everyone else did. Inside though, he was seething. He'd soon become even more infuriated. One night after returning home from the victorious battle over the Philistines, the "evil spirit" from the Lord overcame Saul yet again, and the young shepherd was called one more time to play his instrument for the king. Yet, unlike those first few times, Saul wasn't sleeping restlessly in another room. This time, Saul was engaged.

The king says to himself, "If I can't kill David myself, I'll get him killed on the battlefield." So he appointed the teen-ager captain over a squadron of soldiers and sent him on the most dangerous of missions. In Saul's mind, the boy had gotten lucky once with the giant, but surely there was no way he could survive in a real battle with a real army of enemy soldiers.

Saul didn't know what we know all these years later: David was simply a magnet for the supernatural. Music, lions, bears, Goliath... God was steering David through it all, including the battles Saul intended to be the death of David. In fact, not only was David surviving it all, but with each victory David increased both his following and his fame. Everyone wanted to stand with the kid who always won.

MARRYING A PRINCESS

Saul hasn't forgotten his promise to give his daughter in marriage to the soldier who brought down the Philistine champion. Not surprisingly, one of his daughters, Michal, has fallen in love with everyone's new favorite hero. Saul devised yet another plan to end David's kingdom before it even begins.

One day, Saul sends some of his men to young David. They pat David on the back and pretend to affirm him. "Has the king told you lately how much he appreciates you? He wants you to become his son-in-law."

David had, of course, earned the king's daughter's hand in marriage when he killed Goliath. He had every right at this point to say, "It's about time! I was wondering if King Saul was going to be a man of his word." But that wasn't in David's nature. His genuine humility and grace were an important part of what made him so appealing.

LESSON FROM OLD DR. MARK

Jealousy, envy, and hatred have no rational boundaries. If someone hates you unreasonably or is envious of you, the better you act, the more mature and restrained you become, the more they will hate you. Continue to do the right thing, but know that doing so may not win over your enemies.

David humbly says, "I'm not worthy to marry such a princess. I could never be the king's son-in-law! I'm just a poor nobody, a shepherd. Anyway, there's no way I could ever afford the bride price for the daughter of a king."

Saul's men smile because the naïve fool has taken the bait just as the king suspected he would. They quickly respond, "The king thought about that, and he concluded that a fair bride price would be for you to personally kill and circumcise one hundred Philistine soldiers. When you bring him their foreskins, he'll give you his daughter."

You read that right. Kill one hundred Philistines and then take their foreskins.

"Only one hundred?" David says. "Let's make it an even two hundred."

David is not being smug or arrogant. He is sincerely hoping to show Saul that he is trustworthy, the kind of servant, or son-in-law, who will go beyond, who will eagerly do more than the minimum.

A more distasteful scene can hardly be imagined than the moment when David dumps two hundred bloody foreskins at Saul's feet. Still, it happened. It's right there in 1 Samuel 18. I warned you. This is three thousand years ago, not Buckingham Palace. This didn't happen in the environs of a modern monarchy. "Your Highness, I present to you Sir David, who would like to offer you this chest filled with gold in exchange for your daughter's hand." Hardly!

Even so, that misses the point—the point being David's ability, regardless of Saul's efforts to get him killed, to go on in God's power from victory to victory.

THE UNWITTING SPY

Our modern ideas of marriage simply will not fit into the turbulent and primitive times at the end of the Bronze Age. It is challenging to the modern reader to understand ancient customs, such as multiple wives, concubines, and a bride price. Surely it is clear by now: David is not a twenty-first-century Christian. He lived three thousand years ago. In those days, if a father said, "You can marry my daughter if you bring me a hundred Philistine foreskins," then that was the deal. There was no eloping or ignoring the bride price. There was never a question about what the girl wanted. Did he want to marry her, and could he pay the fee stated in the brochure? In fact, it did not always matter what the prospective groom wanted. Arranged marriages, arranged by the two sets of parents, were the rule rather than the exception.

The difference was that David was a bit of a rock star. The girls swooned over him, including Saul's daughter Michal. She told her dad she'd love to marry David because she had fallen for him.

Saul's devious mind moved into high gear. He determined to manipulate his own lovestruck daughter. From the moment of the marriage, Saul began to pump Michal for information. She was Saul's spy and didn't even know it. Michal was a tragic figure in David's story, and her tragedy began with spying and ended in bitterness.

From the beginning of the relationship, the entire marriage was corrupted because of a divided loyalty in Michal's heart. Michal became a pathetic pawn in a historical nightmare. It wasn't her fault entirely, but in the end she chose loyalty to her father over loyalty to her husband, and she paid a dear price.

Saul's son Jonathan, however, was no Michal—and no Saul. Jonathan was an admirable man, a truly decent man who became David's best friend.

LESSON FROM OLD DR. MARK

Ladies, you will never become a queen if you can't quit being a princess. At some point, you have to shift from being daddy's little girl to being your husband's wife. If you don't, your marriage will never be on solid ground.

THE LOVE OF A FRIEND

I have spent a great deal of my life in Africa. One Sunday night after preaching in Obuasi, the pastor took my hand and held it as we walked to the cars. Whoa! I was not comfortable with that, but I tried not to let my expression give me away. After the pastor left, I asked our Ghana director about it, and he quickly called me out for letting the Western world's obsession with sex keep me from understanding friendship. "He's just walking with you and showed you friendship by taking your hand," he explained to me. "It was not sexual. It was friendship."

This pesky Western mentality hinders us from understanding and appreciating David and Jonathan's friendship. C. S. Lewis, in his book *The Four Loves*, says that the love shared by people in a friendship is considered of little value in the modern world, if it is considered at all. He explains two people in love are absorbed with each other, while friends link arms and move together toward a common good; friends stand shoulder to shoulder in pursuit of a shared vision.[1] David and Jonathan had that kind of love between them. First Samuel 18:1–4 says, "There was an immediate bond between them, for Jonathan loved David.... Jonathan made a solemn pact with David, because he loved him as he loved himself. Jonathan sealed the pact by taking off his robe and giving it to David, together with his tunic, sword, bow, and belt."

There was never any hint whatsoever of homosexuality between these two young men. They genuinely loved and cared for each other as friends, even to the point where Jonathan disobeyed his father the king when the king sought to murder David.

Saul despised David. He envied David's celebrity unreasonably. Saul, after all, was the king. How could anyone, even a dashing young warrior, threaten the king?

Repeatedly he tried to have David assassinated. Saul never dreamed that David would succeed in the macabre bride price he demanded for his daughter. He was sure David would be killed. Now he has a spy in David's bedroom. His rage and insanity reached a new level in 1 Samuel 20 when he let it all out with Jonathan, screaming at his own son, "You son of a perverse, rebellious woman! Do I not know that you have chosen the son of Jesse to your own shame and to the shame of your mother's nakedness?" (v. 30, NKJV).

Reading between the lines here, Saul was basically calling Jonathan's mother a sexual deviant, even hinting that Jonathan's mother may have slept with David. Furthermore, he was apparently accusing Jonathan and David of a perverse relationship. Saul was insane. In demonic rage, Saul made outrageous accusations toward his own family.

It would have been very easy for Jonathan to back away from David, to put some distance between himself and the young man whom his father made public enemy number one. At some point in all of this, Jonathan realized that he would never be the next king and that David had been given that anointing. That should have been sufficient reason for Jonathan to help Saul kill David.

Yet he never went back on the oath he made to David. He protected David from his father, no matter the cost. He told David, "May the LORD be with you as he used to be with my father" (1 Sam. 20:13). Jonathan refused to let his father's madness ruin the best friendship he ever had, and in return he and David were friends in a way that most of us will never really experience.

Leadership Focus: Seek out and make friends whose lives edify yours.

Those brought up in the midst of postmodern relativism have had drilled into them the popular belief that there are two sides to every story. It's certainly not wrong to fully investigate before determining fault in a matter. In some situations though, no matter what you may have been taught, there are not two sides. Sometimes someone is just a villain, a bad seed. He's not torn, nor is he confused, and he is not "a good guy deep down." He's just a bad dude, like Saul in his later years.

Saul is a demonized, egomaniacal tyrant who is manipulative, deceitful, and violent. David, at least in his dealings with Saul, is a person of honor, character, integrity, and loyalty. David continues to treat Saul with the respect due a king.

With which one would you align yourself? David or Saul?

Seems simple, doesn't it? Yet the world has a way of muddying it all up for us. This is what happens with David's wife Michal. She fell in love with a man of character but would not face the truth about her father. Jonathan, however, recognized both David and his father for what they were. Jonathan and David's friendship was edifying, honorable, and enduring. Jonathan refused to betray David, even to his own father.

Today's young people, especially in the West, too easily call too many people "friends." Just because someone "friends" you on Facebook doesn't mean that person is your friend. Acquaintances are not friends; they are just people you know.

If in your life you can build a very few or even one true Jonathan and David friendship, you should be grateful. Put very little trust in casual "friendships."

Do not easily overlook too much. See people for what they are. Find and be an honorable, loyal, sacrificial friend.

CHAPTER 4

FROM HERO TO MADMAN

Based on 1 Samuel 19–22

T HE NEXT PHONE call can change your life. There is no way to know ahead of time all that will result from every decision we make. Even knowing this, there are still moments in life when we press "pause" on life, take a moment to look around us, and ask ourselves, "How in the world did I end up here? How did I go from where I was yesterday to this moment right here? Something has gone terribly wrong."

Surely these must have been David's thoughts when he found himself in Gath, Goliath's hometown where, by the way, the giant's brothers still lived. How did David come to this: rolling on the floor, foaming at the mouth, eating dirt, drooling down his beard, and babbling like a madman? "How in the world did I end up here? Something has gone terribly wrong."

SHELTERED AT RAMAH

How indeed? David had been married to a princess. He was the king's son-in-law and a celebrated hero who had slain Goliath and hundreds of Philistines by hand. He had also been warned. Saul had tried to pin him to a wall with a javelin. This was David's surest sign that his life was about to change.

When Saul tried to murder his son-in-law, David ran immediately into the arms of Michal, his wife. This was a critical moment for Michal. She had been a spy who didn't even know she was a spy. She was the spoiled-rotten daughter of the only king in Israel's history at that point. Since meeting David, there had been divided loyalty in her heart. Would she remain her daddy's princess or become her husband's wife? Initially, she made the right choice to stand by her man.

"We have to get you out of here!" she says to her giant slayer. "If I know my father like I think I do, he's gathering his men right now and sending them here to kill you." She helps her husband climb out a window and makes a dummy out of an idol and some goat hair to fool the killers sent by her father.

When her deceit is discovered and her father the king demands an explanation, she is given an opportunity to take a stand as David's wife. She could have said, "Why are you trying to kill him? He has done nothing to you except win your battles, slay your giants, and sing you to sleep. He's been nothing but a righteous husband to me, your daughter, and I love him very much." Instead, she remains daddy's little princess and fuels her father's rage even more. "I had to," she tells him with crocodile tears pouring down from pathetic brown eyes. "He threatened to kill me if I didn't help him."

Michal disappears from David's story for many years. Later, much later, living in Jerusalem with her husband, King David, she is only referred to as the daughter of Saul—never the wife of David. She could never quite break free of her father, even when he was trying to kill her husband.

The narrow escape from Saul's killers left David with few options. He decided to hide out with the very man who launched him on this journey. That man is Samuel, who ended David's childhood when he came into Jesse's home and poured oil on David's head.

The prophet Samuel was living in Ramah, just northwest of Gibeah. When David found Samuel and told him the entire complicated story of his life since the anointing ceremony, Samuel sheltered David at his own school of prophets, a mysterious place called Naioth. They both knew that Saul had spies all over the country and that he'd soon find David in Ramah, yet the prophet believed David would be safe at Naioth.

Saul's secret police caught wind of David's flight to Ramah, and the king sent troops to capture him. When they arrived in Ramah, they found David and Samuel at Naioth in the midst of worship. They burst in, drew their swords, charged down the aisle toward David, and...began prophesying!

David, who was attempting to escape, stopped in his tracks when he heard the clanking of swords being dropped on the ground and soldiers exclaiming loudly, "Praise be to Yahweh, giver of all life. We pray Thee to pour down Your blessings upon the anointed one, King David!"

Samuel and his prophetic students continued in prayer and worship. David slowly and cautiously came back to sit by Samuel to listen to the soldiers prophesy over him. He remembered something his father once told him long ago on the day he met Samuel. "If you want to kill lions and bears, this is what happens."

The soldiers returned to Saul and with embarrassment reported the bizarre evening at Naioth. Furious now, Saul sent another group of soldiers to finish what the previous squad failed to do. He wanted David dead, and he was not about to let it go.

Shockingly, the same thing happens! Once again, the soldiers dropped their swords and started prophesying over David. Clearly, this was supernatural protection of David's life.

After a third episode of this, Saul knew he must go himself. If you want someone killed, it turns out it's best to do it yourself. One thing Saul knew. He would not prophesy over David.

When Saul arrives, the Spirit of God came upon him, and he tore off his clothes and lay on the ground all day and night prophesying in the presence of David, Samuel, and the others!

The last time David had seen his father-in-law, the king had tried pinning him to the wall with a javelin. Now Saul was naked on the ground prophesying for David the very future he hoped to end with a sword. "David is the king, the anointed of God…" What must David have been thinking? And what was he thinking the next day when, rather than staying in the place where he experienced such supernatural protection, he fled once again, driven by fear and confusion?

LESSON FROM OLD DR. MARK

Like David, you can find yourself in a truly bad place through no fault of your own. Because no one sins in a vacuum, somebody else's destructiveness can get you in a horrible place. The problem is, we try to fix such situations on our own. The weapons of our warfare are not natural but supernatural. We aren't going to be able to fix every situation by the power of the flesh. Trust God and be still.

David leaves Ramah and goes to Nob, where he finds Ahimelech the priest. David is desperate, and desperate men do desperate things. Sadly, David feels he needs to lie to the priest.

David puts a finger to his mouth so as to signal to Ahimelech to remain quiet. "It's OK, my friend. Don't be alarmed. I am on a super-secret mission from the king. It was so urgent for me to leave town on this mission that I didn't even have time to grab any food on my way out. Do you by any chance have a few loaves of bread? I need to quickly get on with my super-secret mission from the king."

"A few loaves? Why so much?" the skeptical priest asks the king's alleged secret agent.

Clearly, having had time to think through all the scenarios of his deception, David responds immediately, "Oh, it's not all for me. Goodness, no. This mission is not only super-secret, it's really dangerous too. I have soldiers hiding in the woods, waiting for my return. And they're really hungry. So how about it? You got anything for us?"

"The only bread I have here is the holy bread for the altar."

"God will not mind. This is for Israel and my humble, hungry, super-secret soldiers…hiding in the woods."

Ahimelech looks around, unsure. How do you say no to the man who "kills his tens of thousands"? It's for the king, right?

"Sure, sure, I suppose you can take it. Give me a minute to gather it up out of the tabernacle. It was just laid out."

Before the priest could round the corner, David speaks again. "While you're at it, do you happen to have any weapons around here I could use? For my super-secret spy mission for the king?"

"Weapons? You're asking a priest for weapons? You, a spy and soldier for the king?"

"As I mentioned, it was pretty urgent. I didn't have time to gather any food, or any weapons either, so I thought I'd ask."

Ahimelech gives David a surprising answer. "Yes, we do have one weapon. It is Goliath's sword. It was left on the battlefield. Someone brought it here. I suppose it's yours as much as any-one's. Would that meet your need for a weapon?"

The secret agent smiles. "Yeah, Goliath's iron sword and the bread from God will do just fine."

One of David's most unexplainable decisions was to leave Naioth where he clearly had supernatural protection from God, and to do so in such a panic that he forgot weapons or food. Perhaps it was simply that: panic. Having said that, however, David's next decision is downright perplexing.

THE MADMAN OF GATH

Carrying Goliath's sword, our wise and discerning shadow king went directly to, of all places, Gath, the city of Goliath, and—more importantly—home to Goliath's brothers.

What was he thinking? What did he think would happen at Gath? He was the most hated and feared man in Israel. He had killed Gath's most celebrated favorite son and cut off his head. Did he think he would get a ticker-tape parade? Maybe elect him mayor? Perhaps afraid, he thought he was out of options. If Saul caught him, he was a dead man for sure. Maybe he hoped the Philistines would receive him as a Hebrew turncoat. This did in fact happen later in David's life. Whatever David's reasoning, Gath was a bad decision. David's worst decision was to leave Naioth. His second worst was to go to Gath.

Of course, the Philistines immediately arrested David and threw him in prison. He had escaped Saul only to wind up in prison in the very city that hated him even more than Saul did. Out of the frying pan into the fire.

David knew that no Hebrew cavalry was going to charge in and rescue him. He was on his own. David drew on his creativity, which was to be a permanent part of his leadership package. He remembered that the Philistines, not unlike many pagan cultures, feared the insane.

Exploiting this superstition, David feigned madness. He rolled on the floor, scratched at the doors, ate dirt, and foamed at the mouth. It was perhaps the most humiliating moment of David's life, but it saved his life.

David played the part well and Achish, King of Gath, wanted nothing to do with a lunatic. "Get him out of here! We don't want him around here another minute." They drove David out of the city like a whipped dog, a mad dog at that.

Look at our future king now. Right back where he was the night he sneaked out of his window and ran for his life. He was alone, with nothing and no one. Saul has destroyed his reputation in Israel. David has destroyed his own reputation in Gath in more ways than one. He told a ludicrous lie to a priest about a super-secret mission for the king. He humiliated himself by feigning madness to escape a foolish mistake. Fleeing from Saul, David has been operating on his own plans, making decisions by himself.

Now alone, homeless, and empty-handed, David flees into the Judean wilderness. There he finds a cave to hole up in and waits to hear the voice of God.

Leadership Focus: Let God meet you where you are.

Are you beginning to see the "de-comic-booked" David? Are you seeing the real David now? Don't get me wrong. He's still David the Great, but sometimes he could be David the Dope.

The boy who had a strong enough faith to kill lions and bears and giants grew into a young man who sometimes forgot to let God work and instead just kept going on his own. Where was his faith? Where was his discernment, telling him God was keeping him safe in Naioth? Was he listening to God when he thought he needed to deceive an old priest for some food? Was faking insanity and foaming at the mouth the guidance of God on how to get safely out of Gath?

David had lost his focus, had forgotten who he was and whom he served. Alone in the cave of

Adullam, he was forced to get quiet and wait for God to reveal the next steps.

Perhaps David's decisions are easier for us to understand than we care to admit. It's pounded into us constantly to just keep going and never give up. Do, do, do! Go, go, go! Never stop.

It's true that many times we are called to action. God often asks us to go to a new place in life or build something new. However, sometimes God calls us to stop, to press pause, to wait on His next instruction, to be still. If your journey seems to be at a dead end, pause there. Wait. If you are at a fork in the road and do not know which way to go, wait. Waiting is so hard, but it's so important. Wait until God comes to you once again with His next word. Don't start hacking through the woods with a machete. Wait for God to meet you where you are and shine a light on that perfect new path.

HIDING IN A CAVE

In the cave all alone, David writes what we now know as Psalm 142: "Wherever I go, my enemies have set traps for me. I look for someone to come and help me, but no one gives me a passing thought! No one will help me; no one cares a bit what happens to me. Then I pray to you, O LORD. I say, 'You are my place of refuge. You are all I really want in life'" (vv. 3–5).

While David waited in that desert dead end, God began to move. Before long, the outcast who crawled into a cave alone began to get company. Word of his presence reached the towns, and they remembered the future king who knew how to handle himself in front of an enemy. Many said to themselves, "Let's go out to the desert. Let's join David."

Some who came were outlaws. Some came who couldn't pay their taxes. Some arrived who had a grievance of some kind toward Saul. For one reason or another they were people who thought being in the desert with David was better than life where they were without him. Gradually, what assembled around David became a terrifying, dedicated private army of six hundred called *gibborim*—"the mighty."[1]

David heard from God in the desert. He stood still and let God meet him where he was. He submitted to life in a wilderness cave, and God gave him an army. These mighty warriors were ferociously dedicated to David. They had left Israel. David was their country now. They had no nation but David and no king but David. And David had no one but them. On the other hand, they and David were now a force to be reckoned with.

CHAPTER 5

FROM MADMAN TO MERCENARY

Based on 1 Samuel 22–30

A s much as we might want to criticize Saul—and he deserves it—we need to give him credit as well. When he became king, there was no organized nation of Israel. There was no palace, no legislature, no courts—not even a military force except a militia of citizen soldiers. Saul forged a powerful army that began to turn the tide of war against Israel's enemies.

Part of the reason for his success was Saul's way of building his army. Though Saul was a Benjamite, he didn't just fill his army with his childhood buddies from the tribe of Benjamin. Instead, the end of 1 Samuel 14 tells us that every time Saul saw a man who was strong or valiant or a good warrior, he took him into his army (v. 52).

In fact, Saul made his army so successful that it begs a question: Since he was a leader enough to have all the best soldiers across the land fighting in his army, how in the world was he outfought by a desert outlaw with only six hundred men?

It was because David had all the best outlaws. The gibborim were a whole new tribe, the tribe of David. They were outlaws, convicts, and Saul-haters of every kind.

David's warriors crossed every tribal line. There were Asherites, Danites, Judeans, and even Benjamites, but what made them one tribe was loyalty to David. Together these six hundred warriors became a highly mobile, well-trained, light cavalry guerilla unit that was the most effective fighting unit in the Negev, the southern desert area of Israel.

David taught them how to fight ambidextrously. This made his troops a legend in the land and an incredibly difficult corps to defeat. Wounded in his sword arm, one of David's men could change hands and kill just as well with the other.

David's mighty men didn't kill Hebrews, but they wreaked havoc on the Amalekites. Soon David's men became the dominant military force in the southern lands—mercenaries if you will, with no law, no nation, and no loyalty but to David.

Betrayal at Keilah

This small army soon became a small desert city with families and livestock.

They were the tribe of David and their numbers swelled daily. They even had their own priest, a man named Abiathar. He was the lone survivor of Saul's murderous raid on Nob. Saul's men slaughtered eighty-five priests at Nob, along with their wives, children, babies, and cattle. Saul had every living creature wiped out for what he saw as Ahimelech's crime of giving David food and the sword of Goliath. The only one to survive was Abiathar, the son of Ahimelech. Abiathar, like the rest of the refugees, came out to the wilderness and to David.

Word spread across the land that David and his guerillas were able to help Hebrews in need. The first to send word to David about their troubles was the nearby town of Keilah, which was under siege by the Amalekites. When David and his forces rescued Keilah, his legend grew yet again. Now he was not merely a glorified outlaw. He was a hero again.

Free of the Amalekites, Keilah and David's army celebrated together, but behind the scenes the town's leaders were afraid. "We had the enemy outside the walls," they say to each other. "Now we've got David inside the walls. These are dangerous men."

"There's something else," someone says. "Did you hear what Saul did to those priests at Nob after just one of them helped David? We have to get ahead of this. We have no choice but to tell Saul David is here."

The city of Keilah, so wonderfully rescued by David, quickly betrayed him. They sent word to Saul, but before the king's troops reached the town, David and his men were able to escape back into the wilderness. David moved his base of operations to a remote oasis named Ein Gedi, meaning "spring of the kid (goat or ibex)."[1] Ein Gedi is in the hills above a rocky desert near the Dead Sea, the lowest point on earth. This area is one of the most barren wildernesses in all the world.

Saul, believing he has David on the ropes, launched an all-out effort to find him and finish him. First Samuel 24:2 says that Saul sent three thousand "elite troops" from throughout Israel to search for David. Saul's handpicked army, the best of the best from all Israel, now have one purpose: find and kill David and smash the gibborim.

It is intriguing that Saul threw such vast resources into the effort to find David. He was not at war with David, and David was not at war with him. Saul was at war, however, constantly with the numerous surrounding pagan tribes. Foolishly, Saul decided to pull troops from his more pressing wars, his real wars, to pursue his personal vendetta against David. It was unwise. It was militarily deadly, and it was evidence of Saul's emotional instability and desperate paranoia.

LESSON FROM OLD DR. MARK

If you allow yourself to get distracted by egotistical issues, you can lose focus on your purpose and destiny. Saul had been successfully winning battles with the Philistines, Amalekites, Amorites, and Hittites, pushing them back farther and farther and extending the territory of his fledgling nation. Yet out of ego, pride, and fear of David taking his throne, he redirects his troops on a wild goose chase. Don't pursue enemies who aren't coming for you. Remain focused on the ones God directed you toward.

A CAVE, A KING, AND A ROBE

With his three thousand soldiers, Saul pursued David relentlessly. David, still doing all he could to avoid fighting and killing his king and any fellow Israelites, hid in the back of a cave. Saul camped nearby, but try as he might, he could not find David. At one point Saul went into that very cave to relieve himself.

"Here's your chance, sir!" one soldier whispers to David. "The Lord has delivered him right into your hands. End it now, right here in this cave, and the kingdom is yours."

David knew better. Killing Saul went against everything David believed. God had anointed Saul as king, and David determined to let God remove him. Murdering Saul was not what God wanted, and David knew it.

In one of the great dramatic scenes in the Bible, while Saul relieved himself, David cuts off a piece of the king's outer robe. When Saul is a safe distance away from the cave, David runs out holding the piece of robe and says, "My lord! I could've killed you back in that cave. But you are the Lord's anointed king, and I will never harm you!"

Seeing that what David says is true, Saul cries, "David my son, is that really you? I'm so sorry. What's the matter with me? Please forgive me, David." With that Saul takes his army back to Gibeah.

That should have been the end of it. After that, any normal human being would have seen what an absurd, sinful thing it was to ever again hate or hurt David, but Saul was not normal. Saul was an unstable, immature, paranoid egotist. When Saul received word that David and his men were in the wilderness of Ziph, he forgot his remorseful promise to David and pursued him once again.

In yet another of the great Bible scenes, Shakespearean in its drama, David proves his innocence again. One night while Saul and his men are asleep, David sneaks into the camp. Saul and his top general, Abner, are lying inside a ring formed by slumbering soldiers. David silently takes Saul's spear and water bottle and returns to where his troops are hiding.

"Abner!" David yells at the king's general. "You should be court-martialed, maybe even executed. You should be ashamed of yourself for not protecting the king as you were instructed."

Holding Saul's water bottle and spear aloft, David shouts, "Once again, I could've killed you, but I didn't. Give it up, my lord. Stop chasing me. What am I? A flea. You are the king. Go back to fighting your real enemies."

Hearing this, Saul gives the same tired performance. "David my son, is that really you? Oh, I'm so sorry. What's the matter with me? Please forgive me, David."

Yet again Saul and his army head back to Gibeah, and yet again David is David at his best, an athletic warrior, a loyal subject of the king, and a man who feared God more than death.

LESSON FROM OLD DR. MARK

People who are driven by ego and emotion are as undependable in their repentance as they are in their commitments. When someone is driven by ego, pride, and emotion and claims to hate you, hate you, hate you, but then they say they love you, love you, love you, do not be fooled. Never cast your life into the hands of such people.

BACK TO GATH

Confronted a second time with Saul's instability, David realized two things. The break with Saul would never be resolved.
He also knew that he could no longer live from cave to cave. It
was getting him nowhere. Oddly, he decided to return to Gath.
Again. Why Gath? Why go again to the hometown of Goliath
where the giant's equally giant brothers were still living? Why
go where David feigned insanity to escape prison? Why?
Because things are different.

This time David enters the city with a feared military force.
This time David has a bargaining chip. This time the Philistine
king, Achish, wants to use David, not kill him. "Sure you can
stay here in Gath, my boy," the aged king says. "You feeling
better since last time you were here? Seeing you like that broke
my heart. If you need refuge in my kingdom—it's yours. Let's
help each other. Bury the hatchet. You know, let bygones be
bygones. By the way, how would you feel about raiding Jewish
towns in southern Judea? We can share their loot and everybody prospers. How does that sound?"

The wily Achish was interested in more than loot. He
thought that if he could get David to raid Jewish towns, then
they would never take him back as one of their own.

Hiring a lethal mercenary like David was a two-edged sword.
In a battle David might decide to turn on the Philistines.
However, if David's raids killed his fellow Hebrews, he could
never go home again. Hiring David was one thing. Owning
him was better.

This chapter of David's life, his season as a mercenary, is
the least known and least talked about of all. This is because
David the mercenary doesn't fit into the twenty-first-century

Christian box we so badly want David to stay in. David lived and made war in a violent and barbaric age. It was an ugly time. Its morals, customs, and understanding of God and life were very different from ours in the twenty-first century. David was what he was. In this period of his life he sold his sword to the highest bidder and that was the Philistines, Israel's most hated enemies.

At the same time David truly loved Israel. He loved his own people. How could he make this work? If he would not kill Saul, who was trying to kill him, he certainly was not going to kill innocent Jews. David and his men rode north as Achish expected him to, then circled south through the Negev into Amalekite territory. They raided Amalekite towns instead, brought the loot back to Gath, and told Achish it was from Jewish towns.

The plan would only work if Achish never learned the truth. That meant one thing: no witnesses. On these vicious raids, David and his men left no one alive. Not one man, woman, or child. They killed every human being and burned the towns to the ground. This was David the mercenary. To understand David, we must come to grips with this bloody part of his life. David was a warrior, a hired sword in a violent era of history. Now David was not only a mercenary, but he was also a double agent.

David and his cavalry became the most productive raiders Achish had. Achish is certain now. David could never leave him. The Jewish farmers of the south, who were constantly under siege by the Amalekites, loved David even more for wiping out these horrifying pagan raiders. David was now the most famous military leader in Judea, loved by both the Jews and the Philistines. Not so much by the Amalekites.

Achish rewarded David by giving him the town of Ziklag. This was a great turning point for David, his men, and their families. Now they had a home, a place that was theirs. In from the desert and into a real town, David's men gratefully landed in Ziklag.

To their young warrior chieftain it must have felt like his destiny had arrived. Samuel said he would be a king and now he is, if not Israel, at least in Ziklag. For the first time in a long time, David felt settled.

Leadership Focus: Before God's best comes to you, a close substitute may present itself. Beware.

It will not be a bad thing. It just won't be God's best. It is so tempting to settle, to accept second best, and to fool ourselves into believing that God's destiny has finally come to us. We reason like this: This wasn't exactly what I thought God said to me, but it's pretty close! After all these years of waiting, I could get used to this. I'll settle for this.

The problem with settling for pretty good is that it may cause us to miss that wonderful blessing God had for us. When we settle for nearly there, we never get all the way there.

Had David really begun to believe that Samuel's anointing meant God wanted him to be king of some Philistine town called Ziklag? Really? Ziklag?

Perhaps, but if so, God was just about to make it quite clear that Ziklag was not His ultimate plan for David. A year and a half after David's army moved to the town, while he and his men were out on another murderous raid for Achish, Amalekite raiders attacked Ziklag, burned the town to the ground, and carried off all the women and children as slaves. Ziklag was gone with the wind.

The problem with leading pirates is that they are pirates. The greatest danger to the captain of a pirate ship is his own crew. It could be said that David was a pirate captain and Ziklag was his ship.

When David and his men returned from a raid to find Ziklag in ashes and their families kidnapped, the crew turned on David. David was everything to them—nation, tribe, leader, and law. When they thought he had failed them, they were ready to kill him. He was all they had, and therefore he was all they had to blame. In any crisis, people look for someone to blame. When pirates blame the captain, the captain is in trouble.

The Bible gives only this cryptic insight into David's response when his own men were going to stone him to death: "David encouraged himself in the LORD his God" (1 Sam. 30:6, KJV).

We do not know exactly how. Did he pray? Did he remind himself of all the times God had protected him in the past? Probably both of these and more. However he encouraged himself in the Lord, it worked.

Like the great leader he was, he told his men, "We can stand here weeping. That's a plan. You can kill me. That's a plan. Not a good one, but it is a plan. Or you can follow my plan. My plan is dry your eyes, lock and load, and mount up. My plan is find the raiders who did this, track them down, kill them all, *and get our wives back. Then let's rebuild this town. How many like that plan?"*

They found the Amalekites, of course. A raiding party that large, dragging hostages, would leave a trail a city slicker could follow, and David's men were not city slickers. They were experienced, battle-hardened, desert warriors bent on bloody revenge.

They rode so hard that some of the men were too exhausted to fight. David left them to guard the baggage and the extra horses. After dark they hit the Amalekite camp. The slaughter was complete, the rescue was total, and David's heroic status with his men was enhanced.

When they returned to the baggage, the men who fought did not want those left there to share in the loot, but David put his foot down. From that moment on it was David's rule: those who guard the baggage get the same share as those who fight.

What do we make of all this?

1. *When discouragement sets in and the blame game begins, real leaders find courage from God.*

2. *In the face of a crisis, calmly make a plan of action and respond. Make a plan and follow the plan.*

3. *In victory be gracious and generous.*

4. *Don't get stuck in a "Ziklag," thinking it is God's best for you. When you settle for a shortsighted distraction, God can allow*

the Amalekites to wipe it away in the blink of an eye.

Beware of the close substitute, and do not forget God's call on your life that was once so clear. Tell God, "I'm at Ziklag right now, Lord, because this is where You have placed me, but my hands are open. I will not clutch this moment to my breast and scream 'Mine, mine, mine!' It's all Yours. Do with it and me what You will."

CHAPTER 6

LEARNING FROM IDIOTS

Based on 1 Samuel 29—2 Samuel 5

THERE IS SO much we can learn from David. Lessons for life and leadership are on every page of his story. Some of these lessons are about what to do, and some are what not to do. A life as complex as David's is also full of lessons from the people around him.

There are great things to be learned from great people. There are also important lessons to be learned from idiots. Better, far better, to learn from one than to be one and gain an idiot's reward.

IDIOT #1: THE AMALEKITE MERCENARY

On the slopes of Mount Gilboa, the Philistines attacked Saul and the Israelite army. David had made the Philistine king, Achish, very rich with Amalekite plunder. The king wanted him in the battle with Saul. David, however, had made a vow to not raise his sword against his fellow Jews. The tension was terrible, but the issue was resolved without David having to do a thing. The Philistine generals pled with Achish to leave David at Ziklag. They did not trust him as they believed he would turn on them in the battle. Achish yielded, and David was spared from having to fight against his own people.

The Philistines attacked Saul with everything they had, and the battle went badly for the Israelite army. Jonathan was killed, Saul was gravely wounded, and it was obvious the battle was lost. Rather than allowing himself to be captured and tortured to death, Saul fell on his own sword. An Amalekite mercenary thought he knew how to use Saul's death for his own advantage.

This Amalekite soldier finds David in Ziklag and says, "Saul is dead! Saul is dead!"

David asks him, "How do you know that? What happened?"

The Amalekite proudly announces, "I barely escaped with my life after the Philistines attacked us at Gilboa. Everyone is either dead or has fled. Saul and Jonathan were not spared their lives, sir."

Falling to his knees in despair, David demands the soldier tell him how he knows this.

In the misread of all misreads, the Amalekite adds what has to be the stupidest lie ever told to a tribal warrior who has personally killed hundreds of people with his own hands. "I killed Saul myself. I saw him wounded on the battlefield, and I killed him."

David wants to be sure of what he just heard, so he asks slowly, "You killed the king? Is that what you're saying?"

With his chin raised high, the Amalekite said, "I sure did. I know you hated him and that he made your life miserable for all those years in the desert. So I killed him for you, Your Majesty."

"You killed him with your own hand?"

"Yes, sir, with this very sword."

David looks to one of his loyal soldiers next to him and says, "Kill this idiot."

As the Amalekite sinks to his knees with a sword in his chest, David gives him the final words he ever hears. "If I spared Saul all those years when he was trying to kill me, what makes you think that I would want you to kill him? It's against God's will to kill the anointed king."

LESSON FROM OLD DR. MARK

You cannot curry favor with a person of integrity by accomplishing what you think they want in an immoral, illegal, or unethical way.

As David mourned the deaths of his king and of his best friend, Jonathan, Israel was beginning to unravel. The tribe of Judah, David's tribe, pulled out first. "We gotta get out of this. Israel is a lost cause. It's time for Judah to stand alone," reasoned Judah's elders.

They made the obvious decision and headed to Ziklag to appeal to David to come to Hebron and be their king. David was the most accomplished military and political leader in Judah, and he had a formidable army. David accepted, and he and his six hundred men evacuated Ziklag. While the Philistines were still out celebrating their recent victory, David and his men headed up into the Judean hills to Hebron, the tribal capital of Judah.

For the first time since his anointing in Bethlehem, David could officially add "King" to his title. He was no longer a shepherd. He was no longer an outlaw hiding in a cave or a mercenary working for the enemy. He was finally a Jewish king over his own tribe.

IDIOT #2: ASAHEL

Judah had their king, and soon Israel would get theirs. The senior general in Saul's army was a formidable soldier named Abner. At Saul's death, Abner made Saul's son Ishbosheth Israel's new king. Abner's control over what was left of Saul's army was sufficient to ensure no objections were raised. Few if any argued with Abner about anything.

In a skirmish between some of Abner's men and the men of Joab, David's top general, Joab's younger brother decided to challenge Abner himself. Joab was a fierce and feared warrior, but his younger brother Asahel was a lightweight. He was no match for Abner and should have known it. Asahel pursued

Abner, determined to make him fight. Abner urged him to turn back, but Asahel was an idiot.

He wouldn't quit. Thinking he had the older man cornered, he charged at him as fast as he could. Abner, deciding he had no other choice, flipped his spear around so the blunt end was out. The out-of-control Asahel ran himself right into the back of the spear, forcing it through his ribs and out his back. Abner, who knew Asahel was Joab's brother, wanted to be able to say later on that he didn't intentionally kill the boy. Of course, such a subtle distinction would be wasted on Joab.

LESSON FROM OLD DR. MARK

Have a modest and reasonable view of your own skills and experiences. Having a great dream is not the same as arrogant overreach. Don't bite off more than you can chew.

IDIOT #3: KING ISHBOSHETH

If Asahel was a fool, and he was, Israel's young king, Ishbosheth, was a class A idiot. He was a weak king of a war-weakened nation that had just lost one of its tribes.

The best thing Ishbosheth had going for him was that he still had Abner, Saul's top general, by his side, advising him along the way. What could possibly have been going through Ishbosheth's mind the day he decided to accuse Abner of sleeping with his father's concubine Rizpah?

Though a man's concubine was not exactly the same as his wife, she was not a prostitute either. She was accepted into the family, into the home. A king's concubine lived in the same compound with his wife or wives. Falsely accusing someone of sleeping with another man's concubine was a serious matter, and Abner was a serious man.

Not surprisingly, the general became furious with the new king's stunning accusation. "You must be insane! I have never touched your father's concubine. After all I have done for you and your family, this is how you treat me?"

Offended and enraged, Abner goes straight to Hebron and tells David, "I've installed an idiot as king. I'm ready to serve you if you want me."

Of course, David gladly received one of the most respected Jewish warriors in Israel.

LESSON FROM OLD DR. MARK

Do not unnecessarily offend anyone. Do not make false accusations. But above all, do not offend and accuse needed allies.

IDIOT #4: ABNER

Abner was a formidable man of war. His weakness was naïveté, incredible naïveté that made him act like an idiot. Knowing that Joab would want revenge, David sent Abner to Hebron, one of the Jewish cities of refuge. By Jewish law, as long a man remains inside the boundaries of a city of refuge, he is safe from anyone who may have a grievance against him. So as long as Abner stayed in Hebron, Joab could not touch him.

When Joab returned home from a raid and heard what David had done, he was furious. "Did you really welcome Abner? Did you? I can't believe it. He spent years hunting you down. He made that dolt Ishbosheth the new king instead of you—and worst of all, he killed my little brother!" Joab protests.

"He's a great warrior, Joab," answers David, "a great asset to have in these times. Leave it be. Your brother was a casualty of war, nothing more. Abner feels badly about how it all played out. He did not want to kill that boy. Your brother was a hot-head and you know it. I sent Abner to Hebron to find refuge. Just leave him be."

Joab immediately left for Hebron. At the city gates Joab called for Abner to come out to him. All Abner had to do was stay where he was. Like a fool, when Joab called him out, Abner crossed the city boundaries. When he did, Joab plunged a dagger into Abner's ribs, exactly where Abner's spear ran through Joab's little brother. In that dangerous world, trusting the wrong man could earn you an idiot's death.

LESSON FROM OLD DR. MARK

The opposite of dangerous naïveté is not bitter, angry cynicism. It is wisdom and caution. Read contracts. Look at the small print. Do not easily trust. Lay hands on no man suddenly.

IDIOTS #5 AND #6: RECAB AND BAANAH

With the desertion and death of Abner, Ishbosheth was now as vulnerable as a king could ever be. Two brothers, captains of Ishbosheth's raiding parties, Recab and Baanah, conspired to murder their king in his sleep and cut off his head. The two were certain this would put them in good with David. Idiots!

When they rode into Hebron with Ishbosheth's head in a bag, they just knew David will welcome them.

"You did this? You killed King Ishbosheth?" he asks.

Recab says, "Yes. We did it for you. We killed him in his sleep."

David looks to a nearby soldier. "Kill these men."

FINALLY KING

Saul and Jonathan were dead. So were Abner and Ishbosheth. Israel needed a king, and the elders of the northern tribes knew there was only one choice and only one thing to do. They humbled themselves and went to Hebron to plead with David to reunify the nation and become the king, not just of Judah, but of all Israel.

"You're the king. You've been the king since you were a little boy, but we thought we needed to stay loyal to Saul. Now we know. You are our king."

At the age of thirty-seven, more than twenty years after Samuel anointed him in Bethlehem, David assumed the throne of Israel, the throne to which God had called him.

Leadership Focus: There are three things to remember between the announcement of your destiny and the destiny itself.

From the announcement of your destiny to anything that even looks like the early stages of its fulfillment, you may go through wars, setbacks, and lonely caves. You will go through seasons where it looks like your destiny is getting further away, not closer. During this time, remember three things.

One, do today what you have to do to succeed in this moment. Wherever God has you right now, He has you there on purpose. Take every opportunity you have to do today well. Succeed wherever God has you, no matter how far from your destiny you think you are.

Two, try not to make mistakes that will damage your own future. David clearly made his share of mistakes, but he was always confident in God's timing and refused to try forcing God's hand.

Three, keep your heart fixed on who God is. In the complications and valleys, stay focused with God at the center of your life. Be a person after God's own heart.

David's journey to the throne of Israel began when a famous prophet anointed him with oil. Between that night and the throne, he spent lonely days herding sheep, lonely years in a cave, and lonely decades in exile. That hardly feels like the proper path to a kingdom. There's no reason to believe that your path to your destiny will look any better. Do as David did: take refuge in God and in His sovereign plan. Wait, I say, wait on the Lord.

Part II

AFTERNOON

Now David is king. The question is, is he still a man after God's own heart? Given his sins and mistakes, is he still someone we should take seriously as a man of divine purpose?

The answer is yes. David made some highly destructive decisions. He was also the psalmist who feared no evil because he knew the presence of God. Even in his darkest moments, something in David never let go of God, and God never let go of David.

Don't trust leadership lessons from a guy who claims to have never messed up. Trust instead the one who is less than perfect, admits who he is, and finds God's grace to go on. That's David. He sinned. He repented, and his repentance was far from secret.

Chapter 7

WIVES, LIVES, AND COLLATERAL DAMAGE

Based on 1 Samuel 25; 2 Samuel 3, 6

I N THE YEARS after David's first wife, Michal, helped him escape out the window of their home in Gibeah and while he served as king of Judah, David married six more women and had at least six children with them.

As I've said, in order to truly understand this Bronze Age warrior-poet-chieftain-king, we must see him as a part of the era in which he lived. Marriages were different in those days. Certainly, people fell in love. In 1 Samuel 18 Michal told her father, King Saul, that she loved David. When it came to marriage, however, money, prestige, and politics usually trumped love. Often a girl was given in marriage because the father needed the income from the bride price. Today this might be called injustice or even slavery. At that time, it was good business or clever politics.

In 2 Samuel 3 there is a list of David's wives, not including Michal: Ahinoam from Jezreel; Abigail, the widow of Nabal; Maacah, daughter of the king of Geshur; Haggith; Abital; and Eglah. At least one of David's marriages, the one to Maacah, the daughter of a king, was pure politics. It no doubt cost David a hefty bride price initially, but it ended up costing even more later when the son they had together, Absalom, became David's enemy.

Abigail, the widow of Nabal, wasn't the widow of Nabal when David first met her. Rather, it was she who interceded to save the life of her foolish husband from David's vengeance.

ABIGAIL

In the days when David and his gibborim were living in the wilderness, they were, in part, mercenaries who protected Hebrew farmers in the region. Hearing of a huge farm in Carmel with three thousand sheep, David sent some of his men to remind the wealthy farmer of all the ways David had protected him. They asked for and expected gratitude and a donation for their services.

The wealthy farmer's name may be a clue to why things fell apart as they did. *Nabal* means "fool" in Hebrew.[1] This fool had the gall to tell David's team of soldiers and outlaws—dangerous men who literally had Amalekite bloodstains on their swords— "I never asked for David's protection! I don't need an outlaw watching over me. You tell him to drop dead! I'm not paying you a thing!"

David had yet to kill a fellow Hebrew during his lifetime, but Nabal changed the equation. Hearing Nabal's response to David's request, the warrior chieftain says, "Men, mount up! We are about to make a fool famous."

As David approached Nabal's farm in a rage, he was greeted by an attractive woman who had brought wheat and oats for the horses, as well as bread, wine, and cheese for David and his men.

"What is all this about?" David demands.

"This is all for you, my lord. I am Abigail. I am your servant, but I have the terrible misfortune of being married to that drunken fool Nabal. When I heard what he did and how he treated your men, I knew that you were going to come here personally and kill us all. I beg you, sir, please accept these gifts instead and leave Nabal and the rest of us alone."

"Why shouldn't I kill Nabal?" David asks. "He insulted me and disrespected all that my men and I have done to help protect his wealth."

The wise, compassionate wife answers, "I know that you spared Saul's life back in that cave. I also know that you have been protecting the Hebrew farmers like us by raiding and killing the nearby Amalekites. More important than that, I know that God has called you and someday you will be king of Israel. When you take the throne that is rightfully yours, I don't want you to enter your kingship with this fool's blood on your hands. Just like you're letting God take care of Saul, I beg you to let God take care of Nabal."

The woman had spoken so wisely that David took note of her. David and his men accepted her gracious gifts and left. The next day Abigail told her hungover husband about her encounter with the man he had threatened. Nabal instantly had a stroke and fell into a coma. He died ten days later. Upon hearing the news of the man's death, David immediately sent for Abigail and asked her to be his wife. When David brought Abigail home, she had to share him with another wife, Ahinoam. Polygamy is an awkward quandary for those in the twenty-first century West, but it was an accepted way of life in David's day.

MICHAL

Michal was a different story. David had not seen Michal for years, not since the night she fashioned a dummy so he could escape her father's troops. She put the blame squarely on her husband, telling her father that David had threatened her if she did not help him escape. Saul, enraged and eager to humiliate David, gave Michal to a man from Gallim named Palti. It was an illegal marriage since Michal was neither widowed nor divorced, but when the king says, "You belong to this man now," there is nothing to be done. Strangely, after ten years of marriage, Palti and Michal had fallen in love and built a happy life in Gallim. Palti, who was deeply in love with Michal, is a pathetic bit player in David's huge life. An African proverb says,

"When two elephants fight, it is the grass that suffers most." [2]
David and Saul were the elephants and poor Palti the grass.

Though the newly crowned king of Judah had two wives already, including the wise and loyal Abigail, he could not leave his first and now estranged wife in the house of another man. David also knew that this false husband might make a claim to the throne of Israel. David knew the incompetent Ishbosheth was the temporary occupant of Saul's throne in Gibeah. When Ishbosheth was gone—and that was inevitable—the tribes in the north would need a new king. David could not run the risk that they would turn to Saul's son-in-law.

When Saul's right-hand man, Abner, left Ishbosheth to join forces with David, the king of Judah told him, "Now go bring Michal to me."

Abner rides into Gallim, finds Michal with her husband Palti, and tells her, "I'm here to take you back to your husband."

Michal recognizes Abner from his years of service to her father and knows he's not a man to be crossed. Nevertheless, she musters enough courage to play dumb. "This is Palti. This is my husband right here," she tells the Abner.

"Not this man," Abner replies. "I'm taking you to David, King of Judah."

"David? He's been gone for years. I barely remember the man. He's not my husband anymore!"

Abner looks into her eyes and says slowly, "Your husband is David, and this is not a debate." Seizing Michal, he pulls her up on his horse.

The stunned and heartbroken Palti follows after them, weeping and calling out for his wife. "Please don't take my wife! Please. I don't have much, but I'll give you whatever I can. Please just leave my wife!"

Abner stops and waits for the pursuing Palti to get close enough to hear him clearly. When Michal's husband reaches them, Abner draws his sword and tells him, "She belongs to David. She always has. Now turn back or I'll kill you."

With that, Michal is ripped away from the home she built with her husband Palti, and returned to a man she hadn't seen in more than ten years. There is no record of whether Palti ever recovered from this pitiable moment. Later events make it clear, however, that Michal never did.

CHAPTER 8

ISRAEL'S THREE-PRONGED LEADER

Based on 2 Samuel 5–6

NOT A DOZEN miles from David's village of Bethlehem stood the impregnable Jebusite stronghold of Jebus. Rising above the Kidron Valley, this fortress of the Jebusites was so strong that its inhabitants had a saying: "We can defend our city with our blind and our lame." David never forgot Bethlehem, and he never forgot Jebus. He knew it was waiting for him.

It had finally happened. The prophecy of Samuel was fulfilled and David was king over all Israel. God had ruled in the affairs of men. As with all great leaders, the first decisions are the most important. They signal all that is to come. David's first royal decisions were wise beyond his years.

POLITICAL LEADER

Saul, who was from the tribe of Benjamin, had established his capital in Benjamin at Gibeah. Now that David was king, he knew that if he continued to rule from Gibeah, it would make the statement that Benjamin was still the center of Israel. If he remained in Hebron, the capital of Judah, he would send the message to the rest of the land that Judah was now the center of Israel. Yet neither was true.

A new nation needed a new capital, someplace not associated with any of the tribes. But where? What place could serve such a purpose? Where could David establish a new capital that says to all the Middle East, "We are Israel. And this is our capital forever"?

David knew where it had to be. All he had to do was capture a city that had never been taken; no less than David himself was the choice of God, so Jebus was the choice of God, and David knew it.

The Jebusites mocked David and his men from atop their walls as they had mocked all comers: "You'll never get in here! Even the blind and lame could keep you out!" (2 Sam. 5:6). David knew his army could never breach the walls. The way into Jebus was not going to be over the walls but through the water tunnel. Joab and a squad of soldiers went up from inside and opened the way for David and his army. When the brief and bloody battle was over, Jebus was David's. A new nation now had a new capital city with a brand-new name: Jerusalem.

In his wisdom, David the Great's first decision as king was great leadership. He made it clear that the old tribal confederation was gone. In its place was Israel, one nation. No single tribe could claim they were of higher significance than any other.

Roughly 2,800 years later, the United States made the same type of decision when they established their capital in Washington, DC, rather than in one of the states. Virginia donated some land, but the capital wasn't in Virginia. Maryland gave up some land, but the capital wasn't in Maryland. No state could say that they were the capital of the country. There was a new capital for a new nation.

MILITARY LEADER

David knew that establishing his capital within a former pagan stronghold instead of in one of the twelve tribes of Israel was the right political move for Israel. David also knew that conquering the "impenetrable" Jebus would send a message across the entire Middle East. It would strike fear into the hearts of the Amorites, Hittites, Amalekites, and of course the Philistines. Now the nations around them knew. This was not Ishbosheth. This was David, and this was different.

The Philistines, however, were not easily cowed. Second Samuel 5:17 says, "When the Philistines heard that David had been anointed king of Israel, they mobilized all their forces to capture him." They wanted to defeat Israel as they had before and kill David as they had killed Saul. In addition, this was personal. The Philistines hated David more than any man alive.

When he was merely a teen, he brought down their top champion with a rock and a sling. He tricked them, not once but twice. First he escaped certain death by feigning madness, knowing they were superstitious about killing the mentally deranged. Then David deceived King Achish by robbing the Amalekites rather than the Hebrews. By the time the ruse was discovered, David had been enthroned as king over Judah and at last all of Israel. Achish was seething. His hatred was uncontainable. Achish was determined to kill David or die trying.

LESSON FROM OLD DR. MARK

Satan has a personal grudge against you. He absolutely hates you because he knows that you are a child of the King. He wants control of your destiny, and he will hit you with everything he's got. Don't forget whose you are. You are a child of God, and you are anointed by the King Himself.

The Philistines came up from Gath with a huge army and encamped in the valley of Rephaim. They spread out their forces all across the valley of Rephaim. There were so many Philistine tents that they covered the floor of the valley.

This was David's first great military test. If he failed this test, he wouldn't get a second. This was win or die. He knew it. The whole Israeli army knew it.

David's advisers gathered and, as generals do, each advocated for his plans. It is interesting, however, that hearing from God was more important to David than all they had to say. David heard God, and he obeyed.

God told David, "Attack straight up the middle of that valley."

It was counterintuitive, to say the least, but David did as he was told. Israel's victory was absolute. They routed the Philistines.

Achish was incensed. In his hatred for David, he was determined to attack again. "Now we know what David will do. Let's go back there and camp once again in the valley. We'll wait for him to charge at us through the middle, but this time we'll open up our ranks, let him come into the middle of us, and then close back on him and kill him."

The Philistines spread their tents as planned. David's generals, with their newfound confidence from the last victory, were eager to attack just as before.

"No," David said, "Not like that. Not this time. I heard from God, and He gave me fresh orders. A new battle, new orders."

LESSON FROM OLD DR. MARK

Not only must you always listen to God, you must always listen for creative variations in His word to you. Just because you did something one way last time under the direction of God doesn't mean that doing it that same way next time is the direction of God. A new business calls for new strategies. A new church calls for new ideas. A new day means new problems and new answers. Listen for God's variations.

God gave David a new plan. "This time they're expecting you. Have your men sneak quietly around the Philistines to that low-lying range of hills back behind the valley. Wait until you hear the wind in the mulberry trees. Then attack."

"God will tell us when to move," David told his men. "When you hear the wind, attack."

LESSON FROM OLD DR. MARK

The greatest discipline of spiritual life is waiting. Even when it feels like the Philistines are bearing down on you and you must attack now, wait for the wind. Wait for the Lord.

When the wind stirred the mulberry leaves, they charged down into the valley and once again wiped out the confused Philistines.

RELIGIOUS LEADER

David established himself as Israel's political leader by making his new capital the old pagan stronghold of Jebus, rather than one of the tribal capitals. By conquering Jebus, followed quickly by the two victories in the Valley of Rephaim, David had proven he was a great military leader. Now David knew he needed to make Jerusalem not just the military and political capital of Israel, but its religious center as well.

The ark of the covenant had for years been stored in a tent in the old military capital of Baalah of Judah. David said to himself, "How can we say we serve the God of Israel unless the ark is here? We need that blessed presence. We must bring the ark to Jerusalem."

David organized a splendid parade to bring the ark from Baalah of Judah up to Jerusalem. The ark was carefully loaded onto an ox cart. An ox cart! David was going to bring the ark to Jerusalem in a Philistine invention. David intended to bring the ark of the covenant to Jerusalem in the same way he carried stolen Amalekite loot to the Philistine capital. "Let's go down to Baalah of Judah and bring the ark of the covenant to Jerusalem!"

Bringing back the ark was a good decision, the right decision, but David didn't do it God's way. The ark of the covenant was never supposed to be carried on an ox cart; it was supposed to be carried on the shoulders of priests.

When the ox cart lurched in a creek bed, causing the ark to wobble, a well-intentioned man named Uzzah foolishly put out his hand to steady the ark. The Scriptures say, "Then the LORD's anger was aroused against Uzzah, and God struck him dead because of this. So Uzzah dies right there beside the Ark of God" (2 Sam. 6:7).

David was confused. He was trying to do God's will. So was Uzzah. Uzzah's motives were pure, yet he ended up dead in a creek bed in the middle of David's parade.

David realizes he can go no farther. He looks about and sees a farmer beside the road. "What's your name?" he asks the stunned man.

"Obed-edom," the man said nervously.

"Well, Obed-edom, the ark of God is about to dwell in your home."

Leadership Focus: God doesn't need you to prop Him up.

> *It would be easy to hear this story of Uzzah and the ark and accuse God. Uzzah was just trying to help, right? He didn't want the ark of the covenant to get all muddy. What's the harm in that? The harm is*

this: God doesn't need your help. You don't need to prop Him up. He props you up.

Propping God up has been one of the major pit-falls in the evangelical community: embroidering testimonies, exaggerating miracles, leaving out details, and cutting corners. God doesn't need us to prop Him up or help Him save face. He's got it all under control.

He doesn't need a Philistine invention to carry His power, and He doesn't need a helping hand. God can take care of Himself.

BRINGING THE ARK TO JERUSALEM

Later, David remembered the ark of God and that disastrous day when the outbreak of God's wrath killed Uzzah. David still longed for the ark to come to Jerusalem, but the terrible question remained: Is it safe?

David sent men to the house of Obed-edom. He was eager for a report. He imagined that all of Obed-edom's household might be dead. It was not too much of a stretch to believe that God had struck them dead just as he had Uzzah. David had heard nothing from Obed-edom since the day Uzzah died.

When his men returned, David asks if those in Obed-edom's household were dead. The captain shook his head, half in joy and half in disbelief. "Your Majesty, they're not dead at all. It is just the opposite. His fields have more bushels per acre than all the fields around him. Where there is drought all around, his fields are getting rain. His vines are filled with grapes, his silos are bulging with wheat, his cattle have more milk than I thought possible, and his wife is pregnant with twins! They have truly been showered with an abundance of God's blessings."

David knew what must be done. He knew that the blessing the ark brought to the household of Obed-edom must come to Israel. It was time to retrieve the ark. This time though, he left the ox cart behind. This time he did it God's way.

LESSON FROM OLD DR. MARK

At times we may be tempted to reject the supernatural power of God out of fear of the unknown, then seek it again during times of need. We can't park God's power in a farmer's barn just because we don't understand it or because we're afraid of it. That's the same as trying to control God. Let God do what He wants to do, and let Him do it His way. He is a God of blessing and abundance. Don't hide Him in a basement because you are afraid of the unknown.

Imagine the scene. This time, David gets it right. Rather than loading the ark of the covenant on an ox cart, the priests carried it as they should. There was worship and dancing and praise. God truly was enthroned once again on the praises of His people.

As the ark neared Jerusalem, David was overcome in the power of the Spirit and began to dance. He did so with such abandon that he cast off his outer garments and danced unashamedly in only a linen ephod—no more than a light shirt and undergarments. He didn't care. He was filled with awe and joy for the presence and power of God that had come into the city he loved. Everything that had happened since the day Samuel first came to Bethlehem had led to this moment. Despite all the running and hiding and bloodshed, this great blessing from God made it worth the years of sacrifice. All David could do at this joyous, holy moment was dance.

LESSON FROM OLD DR. MARK

Nowhere in this passage do we read that David is making others dance. The joy and blessings of that day were for everyone, not only David, yet David never demands that others worship the same way he does. Everyone worships and rejoices differently. Some dance. Some clap their hands. Some raise their hands. Some fold their hands and stay seated. That is the freedom we have in the Spirit of the Lord—to worship however we see fit.

After the ark was placed in the special tent David had prepared for it and burnt offerings were made to the Lord, David's joyful day continued. Second Samuel 6 says that David gave gifts to every man and woman in Israel (v. 19). To everyone he saw, David gave a piece of meat, a loaf of bread, and a jug of wine.

When the party of the century was over, the ecstatic and generous David returned to his home. There he was met by a furious Michal. David was confused. What could possibly be wrong on this glorious day? He was in a generous frame of mind, and he was ready to bless Michal, but she would have none of it.

Michal pours her stored up bitterness on David. "What a pathetic sight! The king of Israel was dancing in the street today like a pervert, exposing himself in front of all those young women! How could you disgrace yourself like that? You disgraced me, and you disgraced Israel."

Michal cannot bring herself to rejoice with her husband. She takes no delight in this historic moment for Israel. Her emotions are all tangled up. She once loved David, but she also once loved Palti. She also loved her vengeful, demonized father, perhaps more than anyone else in her life. To her detriment, her love and devotion to her father, even after his death, will not allow her to find joy in her new life as a queen.

Stung by the contempt spewing from his wife, David says, "That's not what you're angry about. You're not angry that I danced in front of all those people. You're still angry because God removed your father from the throne and put me there in his place. You're a bitter woman who cannot quit being the daughter of a king in order to become the wife of one. God placed me as ruler over Israel, and if I want to dance before the Lord, I will dance before the Lord. I will do it joyfully. If you think that makes me look foolish, then so be it. I will dance like a fool if the Spirit leads me to do such things."

Michal stands in stunned silence as David continues.

"As for those young women who saw me dance, they do not hate me. They do not despise me. They hold me in honor because they know my act of worship was genuine, not perverse. But my wife—my wife is ashamed of her husband the king."

The Scriptures close out this scene with one sentence. "So Michal, the daughter of Saul, remained childless throughout her life" (2 Sam. 6:23).

We don't know exactly what this means. Perhaps Michal's sourness and bitterness of spirit simply dried her up as a woman. Or maybe David told her bluntly, "I don't need you," and never had sex with her again. After all, the man was not short of wives.

What we do know is she never had a child. Though she was the daughter of a king, as well as the wife of a king, she would never be the mother of a king.

Leadership Focus: Though you cannot control the suffering inflicted on you by others, you can control your response to it.

Our hearts go out to Michal. She was something of a pawn in the political chess game between two powerful giants. Though she was in love with David and he with her when they were younger, Saul used her badly. He made her his spy, his unwitting accomplice in a conspiracy against David. Michal would love much, suffer much, and mourn much in her life.

There is also much to learn from Michal. There will be pain in our lives. Events over which we have no control can happen. What we can control is how we respond. We can allow bitterness to take root and dry us up, or we can choose to trust God, praise Him, and experience His joy.

What if David's relationship with Michal had gone differently? What if Michal had said to herself, "My father was wrong, and now he's gone. Now I live with David. Sure, I was given to him twice and lost another man whom I loved. Nevertheless I am David's queen, and he is my king. My husband is in the Spirit of God and is blessed to see the ark of the covenant in Jerusalem. I choose to love this man with all my heart and make our home a happy one"?

If only Michal, instead of spewing venom at her husband, had hurled herself into his arms, kissed him on the mouth, and said, "I saw you dance before the Lord today, and I'm proud to have a man who loves God more than I do. Oh, how I love you!"

If only.

Perhaps the passage that tells us she never had children would never have been written. Perhaps her son would have built God's temple. Perhaps we would never have heard of Bathsheba.

CHAPTER 9

THE KRYPTONITE OF A WUNDERKIND

Based on 2 Samuel 7–8, 10

B ATHSHEBA EVENTS" ARE tragedies for everyone involved, but they don't just happen in the blink of an eye. They don't come out of nowhere like a deer running across the highway and turn life upside-down. They are the result of a series of decisions. The precise moment it happens is a terrible explosion of grief and unhappiness, but that explosion has been coming for a long time. The most notorious affair in history, biblical or secular, is David's with Bathsheba. It looks like an isolated moment, a split second of weakness that was more spontaneous combustion than calculated sin. In part that is true, but there is far more to it than that.

Think about David's life up to this point. Think of all that he had done and become. Today we may refer to someone as a "jack of all trades, master of none," but David was more the opposite—a master of all trades, jack of none.

David came from nothing, the youngest son of an extremely ordinary family. They were not even from the tribe of Benjamin, the warrior tribe. Where did David learn military strategy? Where did he learn the sophisticated tactics he used in battle? How did David learn to play the lyre? Who taught him to write poetry? "The LORD is my shepherd; I shall not want. He maketh me to lie down in green pastures: he leadeth me beside the still waters. He restoreth my soul: he leadeth me in the paths of righteousness for his name's sake" (Ps. 23:1–3, KJV). Who writes that kind of stuff?

David was a multifaceted genius and a nationwide celebrity at a very young age. David was king at age thirty and already the most feared warrior in the land. Stardom at a young age can have its consequences. Too much, too soon can be a pathway to pain.

Many years later, after David's death and when Solomon was king, Solomon wrote, "Pride goes before destruction" (Prov. 16:18). I wonder if Solomon had his father in mind when he penned those words.

Not a Temple Builder

David's early life was replete with rich, amazing stories. He killed lions and bears with his hands. He brought down a giant with a rock. He sang a king to sleep, circumcised two hundred Philistines, was supernaturally protected in Naioth, and became the Philistines' most successful warrior.

Upon becoming king by conquering Jebus and making the fortress his new capital, David quickly established Israel as a force to be reckoned with in the Middle East. Then he brought the ark into Jerusalem so that God's blessings would continue to flow upon his nation. Still only in his thirties, King David was on top of the world and felt unstoppable. Young people often feel bulletproof or, in David's case, arrow proof.

That's a dangerous place for a man of God to be.

At every new level, there is a new devil, and in this middle part of his life David was about to encounter some new and deadly devils.

Second Samuel 7 opens by saying that "the king sat in his house" (v. 1, KJV). This seemingly throwaway phrase in scripture truly signals a turning point in David's life. He was no longer a shepherd boy guiding his sheep. He was not the horseback warrior chasing down evil enemies. He was not the feared outlaw in a desert cave, nor the guerilla raider running the Amalekites out of town. He was a king sitting in his palace. Finally there was peace and prosperity in the land and a new sense of significance for the young king.

It was in this condition of life and heart that David summoned the prophet Nathan.

"Here I have this beautiful palace to live in," David begins telling Nathan, "while the ark of the covenant is still being housed in what amounts to an oversized tent. That doesn't seem right to me on any level. Don't you think it would be a good idea for me to build a temple for the ark?"

Uncharacteristically, Nathan responds immediately, "Yes, that's a great idea! You should build that temple. God is with you on this."

LESSON FROM OLD DR. MARK

Be slow to speak for God. If you have a word from God, then by all means speak it. Be careful though not to respond out of your emotions. Wait for a firm answer from God.

Later that night, however, God reminded Nathan how being a prophet works: first God talks, then the prophet—not vice versa:

> Go and tell my servant David, "This is what the LORD has declared: Are you the one to build a house for me to live in? I have never lived in a house, from the day I brought the Israelites out of Egypt until this very day. I have always moved from one place to another with a tent and a Tabernacle as my dwelling. Yet no matter where I have gone with the Israelites, I have never once complained to Israel's tribal leaders, the shepherds of my people Israel. I have never asked them, 'Why haven't you built me a beautiful cedar house?'"
>
> Now go and say to my servant David, "This is what the LORD of Heaven's Armies has declared: I took you from tending sheep in the pasture and selected you to

be the leader of my people Israel. I have been with you wherever you have gone, and I have destroyed all your enemies before your eyes. Now I will make your name as famous as anyone who has ever lived on the earth! And I will provide a homeland for my people Israel, planting them in a secure place where they will never be disturbed. Evil nations won't oppress them as they've done in the past, starting from the time I appointed judges to rule my people Israel. And I will give you rest from all your enemies.

"Furthermore, the LORD declares that he will make a house for you—a dynasty of kings! For when you die and are buried with your ancestors, I will raise up one of your descendants, your own offspring, and I will make his kingdom strong. He is the one who will build a house—a temple—for my name. And I will secure his royal throne forever. I will be his father, and he will be my son. If he sins, I will correct and discipline him with the rod, like any father would do. But my favor will not be taken from him as I took it from Saul, whom I removed from your sight. Your house and your kingdom will continue before me for all time, and your throne will be secure forever."

—2 SAMUEL 7:5–16

None of what God spoke through Nathan is a rebuke. God's word to David is more of a loving warning from Father to son: "Listen, if you build Me a house, it may be the final blow, the final nail in your coffin of hubris. After all I've already done through you, this thing you must leave for another to do. You don't build Me a house; I build you a house."

Always overflowing with grace, God also reminded David of the long-term blessing that was his. He told David, "I've made your name among the great. Your name will be famous till the end of time." Perhaps David the Great is not too extravagant a title after all. When God says "great," He means "great," and who are we to argue?

It was God who gave David the anointing to kill Goliath. It was God who raised David up from the barley fields of Bethlehem to a palace in Jerusalem. It was God who led David's armies through all those battles. It was God who made the name of a shepherd boy great among the nations.

LESSON FROM OLD DR. MARK

God may well call us to face great challenges, or do great feats for Him, or overcome great obstacles. However, if you get yourself in that place where you think you're building houses for God, He will firmly, sometimes painfully, remind you that He is the one building houses for you. You don't raise Him up; He raises you up.

As though God's word of grace and reassurance to David wasn't incredible enough, He followed it with a wonderful "however." "However, when you die, I will allow your son to build just such a temple." Sometimes God allows a second generation of leadership to accomplish the dream of the previous leader.

God reserved this great accomplishment for David's son—not out of punishment or spite, but out of love. God is extremely aware of the pride men can feel when they survey all that they have supposedly accomplished. God would leave the temple for another king to build. David's pride and the destruction it would bring would certainly mount up in other ways, but the temple was for Solomon to construct.

EXTENDING THE BORDERS

As King David built Israel's military into a substantial force, he began extending his kingdom. He knew that if the tiny country remained the size it was, Israel would forever be fighting defensive wars, both militarily and politically. David knew that Israel must expand and push back their enemies even further.

LESSON FROM OLD DR. MARK

If you camp only on what you already have, you'll be constantly on the defensive. Press out, push the borders, stretch your tent pegs. Go further. Certainly there need to be times of rest, but there also must be seasons of attack. Pause if you must. Solidify your gains from time to time. Then get up and go again. Great leaders always push forward. If you're constantly in a defensive posture, you will constantly remain under attack.

David began moving out against all the surrounding nations that had opposed him: Moabites, Edomites, Hittites, Jebusites, Ammonites, Philistines, and Amalekites. Since Israel was still surrounded by all these enemies, David said, "I'm not going to just sit here in Jerusalem and wait for them to attack me. I'm going after them."

In 2 Samuel 8, we get the full recap of David's border-extension campaign. Verse 3 says that he "destroyed the forces of Hadadezer son of Rehob, king of Zobah, when Hadadezer marched out to strengthen his control along the Euphrates River." So Hadadezer made a power move, and David destroyed him. David extended his kingdom up the Euphrates, nearly to what is now Iraq, crippling his enemies in the north. He captured a thousand chariots, seven thousand horsemen, and twenty thousand foot soldiers, and he hamstrung all but one hundred chariot horses, which he kept for himself.

David was both feared and hated by the nations surrounding Israel. Their leaders recognized the new nation's strength and decided to pursue peace with its young, unpredictable king. King Toi of Hamath, a longtime enemy of Hadadezer, was among those who realized it was healthier to be David's friend than his enemy. Knowing that "the enemy of my enemy is my friend," Toi sent gifts of gold, silver, and bronze to David. The young king of Israel was not only defeating enemies; he was making political allies. He was solidifying his kingdom at the diplomatic level as well.

David next moved south against Edom, where he killed eighteen thousand of their finest soldiers and placed garrisons throughout their nation. He made servants of all their citizens as well. David's name became famous wherever he went because the Lord gave him unprecedented victories, and with every victory came new borders. David the Great was making his mark, and he did so with both mercy and an uncomfortable bloodthirst.

When the king of the neighboring Ammonites died, David decided that he would reach out to the new king, Hanun, because his father, King Nahash, had shown friendship to David. When David sent emissaries to Hanun to express his sympathies for the death of his father, Hanun accused them of being spies. King Hanun sent the emissaries away humiliated, with their beards shaved in half and their robes cut off at the waist.

Hanun tried to dig himself out of this diplomatic disaster quickly by seeking allies and hiring mercenaries. He reinforced his army with twenty thousand Aramean mercenaries, one thousand soldiers from Maacah, and twelve thousand from Tob.

Led by Joab, the Israelite army attacked this army of allies with a predictable ferocity, and the Ammonites and their allies quickly surrendered to Joab and David. Once a fierce army, they now became servants of Israel.

In one battle against the Moabites, David was not as diplomatic or as merciful as he was with Hanun. After conquering Gath first, the largest Philistine city, and then the land of Moab, David knew that if he released the surviving soldiers, he would have to deal with them again later. He did not want to fight the same army twice. He had them all lie down shoulder to shoulder. He took a length of string and laid it long ways across the line of soldiers. David's men killed all the enemy soldiers under the string. Using this dreadful selection method again and again, they decimated the Philistines. Every third group under the string was spared. In other words, two-thirds of the Philistine soldiers were killed. One-third was spared and sent home, too scared to ever face Israel again.

This arbitrary method of deciding executions may seem brutal and heartless to us today, but it was typical of the age in which David reigned. Israel's enemies literally wanted Israel annihilated from the map. They didn't want to just be stronger than David or rule over him; they wanted him and his people wiped off the face of the earth. Israel was fighting for its survival.

Even in this though, David was showing mercy to his enemies. He didn't want the nation he had conquered to be totally depopulated. He didn't want the Philistine women to be unable to bear children for a whole generation. He just needed to make sure their army had been significantly weakened to prevent them from attacking him again.

After David achieved these stunning victories, no enemies of note remained on Israel's borders. He had devastated the Amalekites. He had broken the back of Philistine oppression. He had defeated his enemies all the way to Damascus and even to the Euphrates River in the north. He had smashed the axis powers of Ammon, Assyria, and Moab as well.

While still in his thirties, David had established himself as the preeminent political and military leader of the Middle East. The favor of God surely rested on David. Seasons of undiluted success are wonderful, of course. They can also be dangerous.

Anyone who achieved all David had since he was a boy would struggle with pride. Highly successful leaders, especially young ones, can begin to feel unbreakable. The problem, of course, is that no one is unbreakable, not even David.

David was never broken in battle, but in the irony of ironies, what finally broke him was not going to battle.

Leadership Focus: In every phase of one's life, one plants the seeds of success or failure for the next phase.

> *Your life in the future will be impacted by the choices you make and by what you learn now. What you learn today about yourself and about life, discipline, hope, truth, character, and God will affect your tomorrow more than you realize.*
>
> *The blemishes we paint over, the cracks we plaster over, and the shortcuts we take so that we never really have to deal with the issue at hand all have the capacity to deeply wound our future.*

At an early age, David became a wunderkind. In his twenties and thirties he was a superhero. However, his pride would become his kryptonite, and God was trying to warn him about it before it was too late. When David said that he wanted to build a temple, God told him, "I raised you up. I gave you victory over your enemies. I scattered your enemies before you. I did this, not you. You have wealth, power, and good looks; you can write music and poetry. If you build the temple, I won't be able to save you. I need to hold you in check."

Apparently David didn't get it. He didn't recognize his undealt-with pride today would wreak havoc in his tomorrow. In the end, he wasn't prepared for what was about to loom up out of the swamp and get him. He wasn't prepared at all.

CHAPTER 10

THE GIRL WITH THE CURL

Based on 2 Samuel 11

I F EVER THERE was a single, defining moment that illustrated perfectly the complexities of King David, it is the story of Bathsheba—the temptation, the sin, the fallout, and the repentance. How could "a man after God's own heart" commit adultery, murder, and high-level governmental conspiracy and corruption?

David is rather like the little girl in Henry Wadsworth Longfellow's poem.

> There was a little girl,
> And she had a little curl
>   Right in the middle of her forehead.
> When she was good
> She was very, very good,
>   And when she was bad she was horrid.[1]

The story of Bathsheba can't be explained away by simply pointing out that David was a chieftain warlord at the cusp of the Bronze Age. The culture of the era in which he lived helps us deal with David's polygamy and military brutality. Adultery and the murder of a friend in order to cover it up are not about culture. They are all about sin.

In the middle season of his life, the Bathsheba episode reveals both the darkest valleys of David's journey and what makes him "a man after God's own heart." Johann Wolfgang von Goethe once wrote, "A good man in his darkest aberration, of the right path is conscious still."[2] David was about to step onto a dark and destructive path, but he must have been aware of the right path. Surely he was, because at the end, later than he should have, David chose the right path.

THE DANGERS OF STAYING BEHIND

Nothing in Scripture is wasted. Not one syllable is there by accident. The first few words of 2 Samuel 11 seem innocuous. "In the spring of the year, when kings normally go out to war...David stayed behind in Jerusalem" (v. 1). With those words David's life begins to unravel. That simple sentence means the king is not where he is supposed to be, and that was the open door for terrible disaster.

This was the first time in David's career that he had not personally led the army. When his gibborim raided out of Adullam and Ziklag, David led the way. When the Israelite army extended the nation's borders by driving out Philistines, Ammonites, and Amalekites, David was at least at the base camp and perhaps at the front. Yet here, when the Israelite military might was at its peak, David remained behind in Jerusalem.

Perhaps Joab and David's other advisors implored him to stay behind. Maybe they told him, "Your Majesty, right now Israel is David and David is Israel. If you get killed in battle, we're in big trouble. Please stay here." Perhaps they were genuinely concerned for him, and he was genuinely honoring the wishes of his advisors and generals. Even so, David was still king. The final decision was his and his alone. If he had wanted to lead his army out of Jerusalem, no one could have stopped him.

David was by no means too old for battle at this point in his life. David was still in his thirties. He was not a decrepit old man, more figurehead than warrior. He was a young and virile leader, too young to retire and too easily bored.

Yet David stayed behind in Jerusalem. Maybe he just longed for a little peace. He had been in one battle after another his whole life. He had been personally responsible for hundreds of deaths, and tens of thousands of others had fallen to his armies. Perhaps David was weary of the bloodshed. Maybe he was ready to let his soldiers do the fighting. He was, after all, a king. He must have felt he deserved some R and R.

Israel was expanding. The ark was in Jerusalem. Life was good for the king who used to sleep in caves. For whatever reason, he was not with his army, and he found himself with an abundance of downtime. Just because David didn't have a war on which to expend his energy, it didn't mean he did not have energy to expend.

LESSON FROM OLD DR. MARK

Downtime is not all it's cracked up to be. I know this flies in the face of much that is being taught today, but we would be wise to remember the old proverb "an idle mind is the devil's workshop." It was true for David, and it's still true for all of us. I have struggled much more in seasons of lonely boredom than in demanding days of hard work. Bored boys can become bad boys. Boredom is your enemy.

There was no question about it. David was bored and restless with pent-up energy he didn't know what to do with. Early one evening he took a stroll on the palace rooftop and saw a beautiful woman bathing on the roof of a nearby home.

This was certainly a moment of temptation for David. What man wouldn't be tempted by the sight of a beautiful, naked woman? After all, David was only human. Keep in mind that temptation is not sin. David was taking a walk and his eyes came across a beautiful woman—there was no sin at this point. Though he saw her and realized how attractive she was, he was still OK. The sin was his response.

LESSON FROM OLD DR. MARK

Satan is not called the "father of lies" for no reason. He, indeed, is the master deceiver. He lies to us on both ends of the sin. He is the one who tempts us, then he wants us to feel guilty for being tempted though we haven't yet sinned. When we do sin, he doesn't want us to come under the conviction of the Holy Spirit. Finally, if the Spirit's conviction reaches us, Satan quickly condemns us.

David's response should have been to walk away. He didn't need to be alone at that time; he needed to be distracted. The temptation in that moment was natural; it was not wrong. David just needed some rambunctious friends around him to drown out the sight of Bathsheba bathing in the moonlight.

Unfortunately, David's response is the wrong one. He asks a nearby guard, "Who is that woman?"

It seems an innocent enough question, doesn't it?

"Who is she? I'm just wondering, you know. She's is one of my subjects after all. I feel like I should know everybody."

How many clothed women was he asking about? Of which kids playing hide and seek on other nearby rooftops did he inquire? Though his simple question doesn't feel like a conscious decision to sin, the moment David sought her name, the outcome was settled. The king's pent-up energy now became his enemy.

"She is Bathsheba, the wife of Uriah the Hittite," David was told. That should have ended it. Instead the bored king sent for her. The truth is that there is probably no reply the guard could have given that would have deterred David from sending for her. His mind was already set. He was told not only that she was married, but that her husband was someone close to

David. At the end of David's life, in 2 Samuel 23, Uriah is listed as one of David's mighty men who fought so courageously for the king (v. 39). While Uriah was in a battle, where David himself should have been, the king seduced his friend's wife. Sin is sin, of course, but David's adultery with Bathsheba was also the betrayal of a friend.

After David sent for Bathsheba, there's an odd, rather matter-of-fact statement in Scripture. Remember, nothing in Scripture is wasted. Throughout the Bible, those words and phrases that seem to add little to the story are important. Consider this strange verse in 2 Samuel 11:4: "When she came to the palace, he slept with her. She had just completed the purification rites after having her menstrual period."

According to Jewish law, for seven days after the end of a woman's period she could not have sex with her husband. She had to go through a weeklong ceremony of cleansing. However, there are countless other stories of sex in the Bible where nothing is ever mentioned about these purification rites. Why is it mentioned here? How would David have even known that she was clean ceremonially?

It is possible to get yourself into such a religious, over-spiritualized cloud that you can justify one sin by satisfying one law. David must have asked Bathsheba, "Have you gone through the seven days of ceremonial cleansing?" That is an astonishing question to ask a woman with whom you are about to commit adultery.

David thought religiously in this moment in an effort to spiritualize something that was immoral. Hollywood's lessons on love are strikingly similar, though they emphasize love, not spirituality. Hollywood says, "If you're in love, then by all means leave your husband and the kids for the new man in your life. If you're in love, it's different. It's not the really bad kind of adultery." To Hollywood, falling in love justifies the sin. For David, making sure Bathsheba was ceremonially clean made it seem less like adultery.

He silenced his conscience, wounded his character, and sullied his reputation, and he did so with a religious question: "Are you purified from your uncleanness?"

If David was bored before that night he watched Bathsheba bathe on the rooftop, he was soon to be cured of that. A short time after his affair with Uriah's wife, word came from Bathsheba: "I'm pregnant, and the baby is yours." David the strategist designed a scenario whereby he could pawn the baby off on Uriah, her husband. He would bring Uriah home from the battlefield for a night so that he could spend an intimate evening with his wife. That would at least get the timing of Bathsheba's pregnancy close enough.

David's plan would most certainly have worked had Uriah not been such a good and decent guy. Uriah's moral compass must have been one of the reasons David thought so highly of this good man. This time, however, Uriah's moral compass was an inconvenience to David, and it was to be the death of Uriah.

After feigning interest in a conversation about Joab, the war, and how everything was going, David gets to the real point of his bringing Uriah home.

"While you're here, you may as well go home and spend some much-needed time with your wife. I bet you miss her, huh? And I'm sure she misses you too. So get on outta here, you ol' dog, and enjoy a night at home."

Uriah has none of it. "My king, with all due respect, I cannot do that. The ark is in a tent. My soldiers are all sleeping in tents tonight. How could I go and lie with my wife in a house? How could I go take a warm bath while my men are sleeping in the cold mud? I could never be guilty of such an act. No, I appreciate your kindness, but instead I will sleep here outside your door and be your personal bodyguard tonight."

Uriah's integrity and loyalty should have touched David's heart, but he was too far gone. Uriah's response gave David time to pause, rethink, and halt the whole process. He could have confessed his terrible sin to Uriah. He could at least have sent Uriah back to his troops and let everything play itself out. But no, David actually tried once again to send Uriah to his wife. Surely a restless night sleeping at the king's doorstep would get Uriah thinking he'd rather be with his beautiful wife. David even got Uriah drunk at dinner on the second day before trying to convince him again to go home to Bathsheba. Uriah still refused to sleep more comfortably than the rest of his men. In this moment, a drunk Uriah showed more integrity and character than a sober David.

Now that's a sobering thought.

As he shakes Uriah's hand and sends him back to the army, David gives him a sealed note. "Please give this to Joab."

"Anything for you, Your Majesty," Uriah answers, then quickly rides out of Jerusalem, anxious to be alongside his comrades once again. The note he carries is his own death warrant.

CONSEQUENCES

It all started out as an innocent walk on the rooftop to enjoy the sunset over Jerusalem. David never intended for any of this to happen, not even seeing the beautiful woman bathing on a nearby roof. Even so, seeing her was not the sin; he could've ended it all there. He could've tapped the brakes, turned around, and gotten the guys together for a card game. Instead, he asked who she was. Even though that was the moment he had decided to sin, he still could've stopped it at any time. He didn't have to send for her. He didn't have to put on the false pretenses of being "religious" about the moment. He didn't have to sleep with her. He didn't have to conspire to frame Uriah for the pregnancy. He could have confessed his sins and faced the consequences. He could have, but he didn't.

Having made all these bad decisions, he now made the worst decision of his life. He ordered Joab to place Uriah at the front of the battle where the fighting was the fiercest and withdraw, leaving Uriah exposed to the enemy. This was the principled mercenary who refused to kill a Hebrew when fighting for the Philistines. This was the fugitive who twice could've killed Saul but held firm to the belief that God would remove the man in His own way. This was the same man who now had an inno-cent, loyal soldier of the highest integrity killed to cover his adultery and the resulting pregnancy.

Maybe all this terrible business was what that woman I met in Israel was thinking of when she showed her disgust that I was writing about "that bloody man!" A multifaceted genius. A musician. A poet. A politician. A strategist. A warrior. A con-queror. A national leader. A national founder. When he was good, he was very, very good. When he was bad, he was horrid.

Leadership Focus: Establish patterns that will keep you moving and productive at all times.

> *"I just don't have the gift of administration," is the whiny excuse of lazy leaders. Gifts aside, there is such a thing as hard work. Great leaders rise early and work hard. There is very little mystery in that, and it has even less to do with giftedness.*

When God placed Adam in paradise, He gave him the job of tending to the land. Work is not part of the curse. Work is a gift. God knew work gave Adam a sense of purpose and accomplishment. Great leaders are great workers.

Your work ethic will have far more to do with your success than your gifts. Learn to work, and learn to love work. Manage yourself before you ever try to manage others.

It was not overwork that brought David low. It was self-indulgent indolence.

LESSON FROM OLD DR. MARK

One common dream of young leaders is a job where no one holds you accountable, where nobody checks up on you, and where there's no clock to punch. That is not a dream. It's a dangerous nightmare.

You need others checking on you, following up on you. You need strict guidelines to keep you accountable and productive at all times. You need a set schedule to adhere to even if you have to set it yourself.

The danger of overwork is real to some extent, but the risk is greatly overrated. The far greater danger is loss of focus. The appetite for lazy self-indulgence causes far more damage than hard work.

David had become bored. He let go of his vision. He lost his focus. He let his boat drift, and he was on the reef before he could stop himself. That's not to make an excuse for him. He chose to ask about Bathsheba. He sent for her, slept with her, and had her husband killed. However, it all started because he lost his focus.

All I'm saying is, if he'd had a hobby, it might've helped.

Chapter 11

YOU ARE THE MAN

Based on 2 Samuel 12

D AVID, THE MULTIFACETED enigma, was like the elephant being described by four blind men. One touches the elephant's side and thinks it's a wall. One touches the leg and says it's a tree. Another one touches the trunk and says it's more like a serpent. The last one touches the tail and says, no, it's a broom.

At this midpoint of David's life, his complexity is confusing. What exactly was David? He was a shepherd. A politician. A leader. A rebel guerrilla leader. A hired mercenary working for the enemy. A unifier. A psalm writer. A husband. An adulterer. A murderer.

How could David, the Old Testament superhero, have his innocent, loyal friend killed just to cover up adultery? A night of passion is one thing. To commit murder merely to save yourself the shame and embarrassment of a pregnancy is sin at a different altitude.

Who is this David whose name has been made great in both religious and secular circles throughout history?

He had an affair, got another man's wife pregnant, had her husband killed, and covered up the entire thing by quickly marrying the grieving widow. Surely King David must have thought he had swept the whole thing under the royal rug.

NAGGING GUILT

What began as a typical evening rooftop stroll to enjoy the Jerusalem sunset from the highest point in town ended up as a murder of one of the king's most loyal soldiers.

David would never have wished this entire episode on anyone, but now it was over. Uriah was dead, and David had married the young widow after an abbreviated period of mourning. The people of Israel evidently accepted that the baby was conceived in marriage. David was relieved. Surely the whole dark episode was over

The intense activity, the funeral, the wedding, and at last the birth of a royal baby all combined to help David put the sins out of his mind. For the most part, David must have thought it was behind him. It was sad and regrettable, but it was over. Yet there was something else. Apprehension gnawed at the corners. Every time he hugged his new wife or held his baby he wondered, deep inside, if somehow, someday, the truth would come out.

Under the surface there was also the nagging guilt. David was a man of God who had committed a horrible sin. He buried it, and apparently he had fooled all of Israel. The guilt must have been overwhelming at times. Every time he passed by the tabernacle of the ark of the covenant, or he sat down with his lyre and tried writing a new psalm, it must have been there. At times perhaps David wished he could invite his younger self into his room at night to sing him to sleep.

LESSON FROM OLD DR. MARK

Many psychologists now see guilt only as a destructive force to be avoided at all costs. In fact, guilt is a gift of God. By God's grace, He burdens us with guilt in order to open us up and prepare us to hear His correction. Guilt is an instrument of God to drive us toward grace. It is proof that God still loves us too much to leave us alone!

Here's the thing about sin though: the postman always rings twice. If he doesn't catch you today, he'll be back tomorrow.

David thought he had avoided the worst, but Nathan the prophet was coming around to ring the palace doorbell.

In 2 Samuel 12, David is in the throne room when somebody says, "Your Majesty, Nathan the prophet is here and wants to see you. He says he has a word from God for you." What must have shot through David's mind at this moment? He has been avoiding God. He's been living a lie. He's been sick with guilt. Now, about a year after his night with Bathsheba, maybe a little less, Nathan is at the front door and wants to have a word.

We really don't even have to know David at this point to understand what was going on inside him; we can just take a look at our own carnality. If we were in David's shoes, our hearts would beat faster, our breath would become slower, and everything going on around us would stand still. For David in that moment, Nathan was the only one in the world.

"What do you want, prophet?"

To David's great relief, Nathan doesn't want to talk to the king about Bathsheba or Uriah. Instead, he simply shares a story:

"There were two men in a certain town," Nathan begins. "One was rich, and one was poor. The rich man owned a great many sheep and cattle. The poor man owned nothing but one little lamb. He raised that little lamb, and it grew up with his children. It ate from the man's own plate and drank from his cup. He cuddled it in his arms like a baby daughter. One day a guest arrived at the home of the rich man. Instead of killing an animal from his own flock or herd, he took the poor man's lamb and killed it and prepared it for his guest" (2 Sam. 12:1–4).

LESSON FROM OLD DR. MARK

A funny thing about human nature—when you feel guilty about something hidden in your own life and God shines the light of exposure on the sin of somebody other than you, you will be: 1) relieved that the light is not on you—inside you will be thinking, "Whew! Somebody else got caught, not me"; 2) the most outraged person in the room. An overinflated righteous indignation can arise from a guilty conscience. "I can't believe they did that! How could they?"

Of course, ultimately this is all just mind games, self-deception of the worst order. Furthermore it will not work for long, if *work* means "silencing the nagging pain of our guilt." The guilt is there beneath the mental rug under which it was so carefully swept. It will not be denied, gnawing away like termites just beneath the hardening surface of our sin.

A story such as Nathan's gives us a moment's relief, but only a moment. Then, there it is again: guilt, refusing to shut its bothersome mouth.

In the end, of course, guilt is not the enemy of the soul but of our soul's carefully constructed systems of denial and defense. Guilt is the instrument of God to burst through the outer walls and storm the inner chambers of our heart, forcing sin to surface, dredging it up and dragging it out before our horrified eyes.

There at last, by the grace of God, we face our sin for what it is. Denial now denied, we must face the truth, just as David did, not because God hates us enough to make us feel guilty, but because He loves us enough. Just as He loved David.

ADMITTING THE TRUTH

Nathan's story is on one hand a wonderful relief to David. On the other hand he is genuinely outraged. The king, overflowing with pent-up guilt, pounds his fist and pronounces his sentence.

"As surely as the Lord lives, this man deserves to die! He can't get away with taking this poor man's lamb! He must restore the sheep fourfold, and after that, he will pay with his life!"

For a moment, everyone in the throne room stands gazing at David, but then Nathan boldly puts a quick end to the silence. Pointing straight into the king's face the prophet shouts, "You're the man! You're the one who stole the lamb. I know what you did. God revealed to me your affair with Bathsheba and your murder of Uriah the Hittite. If anyone deserves to die right now, it's you!"

Imagine the shock, the absolute horror among those in the room. Joab's hand surely went to the hilt of his sword. He was always too ready to kill and would have taken old Nathan's off head with but a nod from David. All David has to do is snap his fingers and Joab will plunge that sword into Nathan's heart. Nobody talks to a king like that, not unless they wanted it to be the last words they ever spoke. David is burdened with guilt over the murder of an innocent man, but Joab certainly isn't. He'll gladly open this prophet up and sleep like a baby tonight.

To everyone's surprise, however, David waves Joab off, motioning him to stand at ease. David drops his head in his hands, and says, "You're right. I did everything you just said. I have sinned against the Lord."

LESSON FROM OLD DR. MARK

Can you imagine how the Scriptures would read if David had looked Nathan in the face and said, "You old fool. You don't know what you're talking about. He's all yours, Joab"? That would have changed everything. In fact, it would have been the end of David. In the crisis the great king's real character shone through. Instead of angry denial he said, "You're right. I did it." Confession doesn't excuse the sin. It certainly doesn't make it magically OK. Sin reveals a man's humanity. What reveals your true character is the willingness to confess and endure the pain.

With David broken before him, Nathan lowers his voice a few decibels and continues speaking on God's behalf to the anointed king. "Yes, you have sinned, but the Lord has forgiven you. Though even according to your own words, you deserve to die, the Lord will not kill you. However—"

A half-relieved, half-sick David picks up his head and looks at Nathan, who is clearly uncomfortable with what he's about to say.

"However," Nathan begins again, "your newborn baby will die."

Some things in Scripture are just hard to swallow—hard to hear, hard to read about. David would've offered up his own life at this point. He was prepared to walk away from the throne. He was ready to confess his sins to the whole world, but not to lose his baby who was the only completely innocent person in the whole situation. That was impossible to wrap his mind around. Why would a baby die because of the father's sins?

Some theological hogs just can't be wrestled to the ground. Not then, and not three thousand years later. David had spent much of his life just trying to survive another day. Now he was going to learn a terrible, terrible lesson. Nobody sins in a vacuum.

When you sin, other people get hurt. Sin breaks hearts. It disappoints. It wounds.

It causes disease, disorder, and confusion. Sin is never a victimless crime. It has consequences that go beyond your own guilt and grief. The people who die as a result of sin are not always the sinners. It is in motion now. Nothing could stop it. The baby will die.

Soon after Nathan leaves, the baby falls desperately ill. For seven days, David prays and fasts, and calls out to God, "It was me who sinned, Lord. It was me! Don't take my baby, please."

It's useless, of course. The baby dies.

LESSON FROM OLD DR. MARK

You can repent of sin and be forgiven, but you may not always be able to alter the outcome. A naughty little boy can pick up a rock and think how fun it would be to shatter a window with it. Immediately after he throws the rock, he thinks, "Oh no. Oh, God, I'm sorry."

Does God forgive him? Of course. Is God going to stop that rock in midair and drop it safely to the ground? Unlikely.

The Scriptures say that the palace staff was scared to be around their king during this pain-drenched time. They tiptoed around, afraid to mention the baby. David's weeping and fasting frightened them. When the baby died, they knew he would be inconsolable. Instead, David's reaction shocked them. David picked himself up off the ground, bathed himself, changed his clothes, and went to the tabernacle to worship the Lord.

After a year of hidden sin and racking guilt followed by seven days of self-denial and desperate pleading for the life of his child, David had come to a moment where he could say, "Yes, I have sinned, and it's all been exposed. Yes, I've suffered, and my child has paid the ultimate price. Now the night is over, and it's time to let healing begin. I'm going to wash my face and find God."

At the end of this dreadful week, God's redemptive grace takes hold of David. David returned to his wife Bathsheba, comforted her, and made love with her, and she became pregnant once again. At the birth of their son, whom they named Solomon, Nathan arrived again. This time his message was not a rebuke. He said God would call their new baby Jedidiah. It is the only time in the Bible the name is used. It means "beloved of the Lord."[1] In other words God said, "You see, I still love you and I love this baby." God showed David both His terrible judgment and His wonderful grace.

God may thrash us. He may chasten us painfully, but He doesn't hold a grudge. God doesn't sulk with you and say, "Now I've marked you off My list; I'm through with you forever." At some point, God says, "OK, I've told you what I wanted to tell you. I've rebuked you; I've chastened you; now let Me bless you in My grace."

Solomon, the future king and builder of the temple, was God's grace to David and Bathsheba.

GENUINE REPENTANCE

Somebody once asked me, "How do you know if a man's repentance is genuine?" One good indication of sincerity is if the depth of the repentance matches the magnitude of their sin. Their repentance may not be as public as David's. That may not be required. The depth, the deep soul brokenness of the repentance is the key.

What could David do to show repentance on the same level as Nathan's public denunciation? He couldn't take an ad out in the paper. A special sacrifice didn't seem right. Abdication? God appointed David, so he had no right to remove himself. There was no such thing as impeachment. How could David not only make his confession public but memorialize it in such a way that no one would ever forget what he did or how he repented?

David the psalmist knew exactly what he needed to do. One day he hands a piece of parchment to the chief musician and says, "I've written a song, and I want you to get the choir together and sing it for everybody. Get a huge crowd gathered for it."

The chief musician says, "Great. Love to. Let's take a look at it."

He takes the parchment from David and begins to read, looking up at his king in bewilderment after he reads the introduction. Awkwardly, he reads the entire psalm before responding:

> **For the choir director: A psalm of David, regarding the time Nathan the prophet came to him after David had committed adultery with Bathsheba.**
>
> Have mercy on me, O God, because of your unfailing love. Because of your great compassion, blot out the stain of my sins. Wash me clean from my guilt. Purify me from my sin. For I recognize my rebellion; it haunts me day and night. Against you, and you alone, have I sinned; I have done what is evil in your sight. You will be proved right in what you say, and your judgment against me is just. For I was born a sinner—yes, from the moment my mother conceived me. But you desire honesty from the womb, teaching me wisdom even there.

Purify me from my sins, and I will be clean; wash me, and I will be whiter than snow. Oh, give me back my joy again; you have broken me—now let me rejoice. Don't keep looking at my sins. Remove the stain of my guilt. Create in me a clean heart, O God. Renew a loyal spirit within me. Do not banish me from your presence, and don't take your Holy Spirit from me.

Restore to me the joy of your salvation, and make me willing to obey you. Then I will teach your ways to rebels, and they will return to you. Forgive me for shedding blood, O God who saves; then I will joyfully sing of your forgiveness. Unseal my lips, O Lord, that my mouth may praise you.

You do not desire a sacrifice, or I would offer one. You do not want a burnt offering. The sacrifice you desire is a broken spirit. You will not reject a broken and repentant heart, O God. Look with favor on Zion and help her; rebuild the walls of Jerusalem. Then you will be pleased with sacrifices offered in the right spirit—with burnt offerings and whole burnt offerings. Then bulls will again be sacrificed on your altar.

—PSALM 51

The chief musician finally looks up to David and says, "Your Majesty, we can't sing this. Everybody is going to know what this is about. We've all been willing to forget about it. Can't we do that? Can't we just forget it? Nobody is talking about Uriah anymore. Bathsheba is your wife; you have a beautiful baby boy. Can't we just leave all this behind?"

David the Great tells him authoritatively, "You will sing it. You will sing it every time I tell you to sing it. When I'm dead and gone, I want you to keep singing it. I want my sin memorialized forever so that everyone will know what I did. More importantly, they will know of my repentance and the grace of God poured down on me despite my wretched sin."

David left his chief musician no choice. Three thousand years later, just as David wished, people still read this rich, profound poem written by a broken but forgiven man, and they are reminded of the depravity of man and the unfathomable grace of Almighty God.

Leadership Focus: Three lessons of repentance from Psalm 51

Heartfelt apologies and true repentance are few and far between. We get denials, lies, excuses, and avoidance, and in the rare instance where an apology is actually issued, it's oftentimes in the form of a 140-character tweet or a half-hearted "I'm sorry if I offended you."

David's egregious sins are not forgotten even three thousand years later, mostly because he didn't want us to forget them. He committed murder and adultery, but his true character, his true heart, is revealed not in his sin, but in the psalm he wrote. In this great psalm David gave us three specific lessons on what true repentance actually looks like.

One, David memorialized his own sin so that it would be known by all who read the Bible until the end of time. He said, "I don't want anyone to ever forget what I did."

Two, David said, "I have sinned. I acknowledge my transgressions." Psalm 51 is all about David's sins. There's no mention of Uriah, how if he had just gone to sleep with his wife he would still be alive.

There is no word about why Bathsheba was bathing naked on the rooftop for anyone to see. In fact, she is not mentioned at all. "I'm sorry, but you made me angry" is not an apology but a veiled accusation. "I'm sorry, but my roommate made me" is a smoke screen, not an act of confession. Confession and repentance should be all about you and what you did.

Three, though David began his confession with the correct focus of his sins, he ended it by turning the attention to God's grace. "Purify me from my sins.... Remove the stain of my guilt.... Restore to me the joy of your salvation" (vv. 7, 9, 12). So much about David amazes us three millennia after his death. Most amazing of all was David's grasp on grace. His theology of forgiveness and cleansing and renewal is astonishingly New Testament in its language and tone. One thousand years before Christ, David wrote as clear a statement of repentance and grace as there is in the New Testament.

Who is this David we have read about for three thousand years? An adulterer? Yes. A murderer? Without question, David never refuted it. Was he also forgiven, redeemed, and restored by God? Absolutely.

PART III

EVENING

———

D AVID WAS A faithful servant to King Saul, a fearless warrior, an anointed musician, a brilliant strategist, a talented poet, and a repentant man after God's own heart—but he was absolutely horrible at family. Even beyond the inherent problems of polygamy and adultery, David's greatest family weakness was his poor parenting. David was a far better king than he was a father.

The final season of David's life is not "happily ever after." His later years should have been years of peace, prosperity, and blessings. He should have been reaping the rewards of his earlier years of sacrifice. Instead, he faced another civil war, this time led by his own enraged and bitter son. Even in the last days of his life he must defang a political plot that is too unreal to have been made up. Finally, from his deathbed David dictated a hit list like a Mafia don. In the last decades of David's reign, he was tested in ways he never saw coming. During these painful years, David composed some of the most heartbreakingly honest words ever written.

Yet at the end, David is still called a man after God's own heart. This must mean that through it all, he truly loved God more than he did anyone or anything else.

CHAPTER 12

PAIN, POLITICS, AND POLYGAMY

Based on 2 Samuel 13–16

D AVID MUST BE seen in the context of the times in which he lived. There is no other way to study David that would be as honest. He was not a twenty-first-century Christian, and he cannot be held to our expectations for a man of God today. He was a primitive warlord at the end of the Bronze Age, the warrior-king of a nation fighting for survival. He was also a polygamist with several wives and even more concubines. There are serious complications in any polygamous household.

Polygamy was commonplace in David's day, but it was never God's best and highest plan for marriage. God had always been clear about His will for marriage—one man and one woman. Polygamy complicates and politicizes everything. The polygamist's family is a swamp of plotting women and half siblings competing for the love, approval, and estate of the man they share.

God dealt with David in the era in which he lived, and David walked in the light that he had, which included polygamy. That does not mean God shielded David from the disastrous effects of polygamy. David's multiple families became the source of the greatest pain in David's later years. The fruit of his polygamous lifestyle would rise up and haunt David and his kingdom for the rest of his life. The worst of it began with a young man's lust for his own half sister.

AMNON AND TAMAR

David's oldest son, Amnon, believed he had fallen in love with his half sister Tamar. In fact, it was nothing more than sexual obsession. Knowing his father would never allow him to marry his half sister, Amnon hatched a pathetic plan to rape her.

Amnon feigned sickness and claimed to be unable to get out of bed. When his father asked what might make him feel better, Amnon said, "If my dear sister Tamar could come by and fix some food for me here at the side of my bed and feed it to me by hand, I'm sure that would make me feel better."

This is patently absurd on its face, but inexplicably David agreed to his son's request and sent Tamar to do as her brother asked. The king had certainly not forgotten the night so many years ago when he "innocently" asked for Bathsheba's name and sent for her. At Amnon's strange request to be hand-fed by his sister, David must have had doubts, an intuitive sense that the situation was not right, that something was off, but he acceded anyway.

David overrode his own doubts and, ignoring his sixth sense, he sent his daughter to his son's bedroom. The horrible result was a foregone conclusion.

After Amnon raped the virgin Tamar, he banished her from his presence. David's virgin daughters were allowed to wear a multicolored gown in public, but Tamar knew she had no choice but to rip her dress in public when she left Amnon's bedroom, a sign that she was no longer a virgin. She begged Amnon to ask their father if they could marry, but Amnon could no longer stand the sight of her and forced her to leave in disgrace.

Tamar also had a full brother, Absalom. Their mother was Maacah, the daughter of the king of Geshur. Seeing his sister tear her robe and put ashes on her head, Absalom tried to console his devastated sister. She told him everything that had happened, and he sent her from the palace to live in his house. Tamar more or less had a nervous breakdown as a young, unmarried woman and grieved for the rest of her life, never again leaving the protection of her big brother's house.

The Scriptures say that King David was "very angry" when hearing of Amnon's rape of Tamar (2 Sam. 13:21). The King James says David was "wroth" with Amnon. This strong word used to describe David's emotions is the same word used to describe Cain before he killed his brother out of jealousy (Gen. 4:5, KJV). The same word is also used to describe Jacob's sons in Genesis 34 when they learn that their sister had been raped (v. 7, KJV).

What did the fearless warrior David do when he heard of this incestuous rape in his own family? Absolutely nothing. While Absalom sheltered his beloved sister, his hatred for his half brother Amnon festered. His father's refusal to punish Amnon pushed Absalom to his breaking point. At minimum, David should've thrown Amnon in jail. By Jewish law he should have been executed. Remarkably, David did nothing, nothing except make an enemy out of his son Absalom.

LESSON FROM OLD DR. MARK

There are times to show grace, and there are times not to. If you get these backward, you will truly damage your own leadership.

With your children, your employees, or others under your leadership, there will be times when you have to be gentle, loving, and gracious. Likewise there will be times when you have to put the hammer down. It is essential to everyone involved that you discern when to do which. The tendency of the legalist will always be to expose and punish every sin. That must be tempered with grace. David's inclination to sweep it under the rug was a disaster.

When leadership does nothing to protect the oppressed, it fuels the anger of those who then take up the offense. After two years of comforting his distraught sister, Absalom's rage knew no bounds. Clearly David was not going to do anything to punish Amnon, so Absalom plotted his vengeance.

Absalom held a banquet one night and invited all of David's sons, including Amnon, to celebrate the occasion of his sheep being sheared for a hefty profit. Late into the evening, when Amnon was drunk, Absalom snapped his fingers and his soldiers immediately stabbed Amnon to death. Panic ensued, and the remaining brothers ran for their lives.

Word reached David that Absalom had killed all of his brothers, all of David's sons. The king was hysterical with grief. He tore his clothes and fell prostrate to the floor. Not long after David received this erroneous message, his nephew Jonadab was able to clarify for the king that only Amnon had been killed. By that time Absalom had fled.

Amnon deserved to be executed for the rape of Tamar, but that execution should have been ordered by King David, not carried out years later by a vengeful brother. Now that one of his sons had killed the other, David compounded his error. David had not fully dealt with Amnon. Now he didn't know how to handle the lethal Absalom.

Absalom's bloodlust would not end with Amnon's death. What happened to Tamar was a horrible thing. David did not handle it wisely or justly as king or father. Still, Absalom took the matter into his own hands and lived the rest of his life in anger and rebellion. In the end, he was destroyed by his own murderous rage. Though Amnon was dead, revenge made Absalom feel no better. He was not satisfied. Now he wanted more blood—David's. Absalom fled Jerusalem, but he spent his years in exile plotting his return and rebellion.

LESSON FROM OLD DR. MARK

A day will come when someone is going to do something you don't like or approve of. Hopefully you will not kill him as Absalom did, but there are other ways you might weave a fabric of revenge, rebellion, or sedition. If you do, this will be the end for you as it was for Absalom. If you build a lifetime of rebellion around somebody else's sins, it will destroy you. The universe is unjust. Life is not fair. Choose to live a life of integrity and character, and life's injustices will not rob you of the healing power of God.

At the end of three years of exile, Absalom launched a campaign to be recalled to Jerusalem. His cat's-paw in this was Joab, which is fascinating. Joab was a seriously lethal human being. If David was Wyatt Earp, Joab was his trigger-happy Doc Holliday. Tender familial compassion was hardly Joab's strong suit. Joab told David, "Listen, I know that Absalom killed Amnon. That was wrong and I hate it, but you can't have your son living outside Israel for the rest of his life. Please consider inviting him back."

David agreed and allowed Absalom to return to Jerusalem. Yet again, however, David's tendency to do things halfway surfaces. He allowed Absalom back into Jerusalem, but not to the palace and not into David's presence. David never fully punished Amnon. Then he never fully forgives Absalom, which would've meant welcoming him back home with open arms. Instead, he told his son, "You can come back to Israel, but I don't want to see your face." Absalom remained in emotional exile, even in Jerusalem.

Leadership Focus: Deal with the issue all the way.

Someday you may have an employee or associate or even a family member who fouls up big time. Seize the opportunity to show them grace if they submit to the process. Hopefully they will, and hopefully they will be fully restored. If so, you will have a devoted friend for life. If not, if they choose not to submit to the process, there has to come a moment when you deal with it—all the way. If you are going to cut off the dog's tail, don't do it by inches.

This can be the hardest thing for young leaders to learn. Sometimes to fire an employee is an act of love. "I love you so much that I'm not going to allow you to go forward in this kind of sloppy, self-indulgent, characterless living. I love you so much that you have to experience this wound."

Firm discipline is important so that the one in need of discipline will not lose confidence in your leadership. Failure to discipline convinces poor employees that you will never follow through. It is naïve to think that overlooking poor performance will change anyone. If they repeatedly press the matter all the way to the red line and even cross it, and you fail to act, they will lose confidence in your own character, and their behavior will get worse.

More importantly, when you refuse to deal with the issue at hand in the appropriate way, other followers will wonder what is wrong with you. They will think that either you can't see the problem or that you deliberately close your eyes to it. Perhaps they'll believe that the person deserving of discipline has you in some kind of a stranglehold. "Why won't the king deal with this?" "Why won't the pastor fire this guy?" "Why won't the president release this person?"

David failed to deal with his children. He never dealt with Amnon for raping Tamar, so Absalom took matters into his own hands. Then David refused to deal with Absalom and allowed Absalom's self-imposed exile to be the solution. Finally David allowed Absalom to come back to Jerusalem but not to the palace. Halfway discipline followed by halfway forgiveness put David's family and his nation in jeopardy.

Don't make the same mistakes. Deal with the issue fully. Firm, robust, and redemptive leadership pays great dividends.

After three years in a foreign exile and two years of silence in Jerusalem, Absalom still could not get over his sister's rape. He even memorialized it by naming his own daughter Tamar. This seems not to have been a sweet, brotherly gesture, but the bitter act of a vengeful man. What Amnon did to Tamar was horrible. Then, tragically, Absalom let it poison his spirit with hatred and rebellion.

Absalom devised a new plan of revenge that could only be fulfilled if his relationship with his father was renewed, but the king still refused to see him. Absalom knew whom he needed; Joab had successfully appealed before, and Absalom knew he could do it again. This time, however, Joab refused to answer any of Absalom's emails. Time after time,

Joab refused to respond. Absalom's solution was to set fire to Joab's barley field.

A confused and angry Joab demanded an answer. "Why did you burn my field?"

Absalom's answer was cold. "Answer your emails."

LESSON FROM OLD DR. MARK

Cold-blooded overreaction is a dead giveaway that something is really wrong. Emotional overreaction is a danger signal. You would be wise to pay attention when someone burns your field because you don't answer your emails. That is a person that bears watching. Something is wrong inside. Ignore that, and you'll suffer for it.

ABSALOM THE DEMAGOGUE

Neither Joab nor David suspected Absalom's real intentions for seeking reentrance into the palace. Absalom's creepy pyromaniac tendencies should have warned them. Instead Absalom was invited back into David's household.

David's oldest son, the crown prince, now restored to the kingdom, wasted no time setting in motion the next phase of his mutiny. The Scriptures say he "bought a chariot and horses, and he hired fifty bodyguards to run ahead of him" (2 Sam. 15:1). On his personal parades through the city, trumpets blew for him and his footmen shouted out, "Absalom is coming!" It was a vain, self-exalting show. Absalom was strikingly handsome, and he knew it. He wanted the eyes of Israel on him, not on David.

When those wishing to bring a case to the king for judgment passed by, Absalom would listen to their stories and tell them,

"You have a really strong case here! Too bad King David is so backlogged. He can't hear you himself, and he won't appoint a deputy to hear you. I wish I could be the judge. I'd rule in your favor for sure."

Instead of being grateful for being allowed to come home, Absalom became a ruthless demagogue. He took every opportunity to cast David in a bad light. For example, he refused to allow people to bow to him. Bowing was the appropriate and accepted manner to acknowledge such a high official as the crown prince. Instead, Absalom would tell them, "My father likes that kind of stuff, but not me. Come up here in my chariot and give me a kiss." This was not humility. He was using this act of informality to make David look bad by contrast.

Likewise, the kiss was not a homosexual act but a Middle Eastern sign of friendship. Absalom was exploiting a natural desire to have a close, intimate relationship with such a powerful and attractive member of the royal family. Absalom also claimed to be willing to fight for them and their causes. Absalom was hardly the everyman good fellow he pretended to be. He was in fact an insidious rebel waiting not so patiently for the right moment to spring his final deadly trap.

LESSON FROM OLD DR. MARK

Do not let yourself become the associate who steals the admiration of the board that ought to go to the CEO. Do not become the youth pastor who steals the heart of the congregation that should go to the lead pastor. This is the inappropriate theft of admiration that should go to your leader. It is seditious, it is rebellious, and it destroys everything in its path.

For four years Absalom stole the hearts of his father's people until at last he knew the moment had come. Absalom requested another meeting with his father and explained to him, "While I was living in Geshur, afraid to return home to Jerusalem because of my great sins, I promised the Lord that if ever I was welcomed home, I would return to our old home of Hebron and offer up sacrifices to Him. Would it be OK if I returned there now to fulfill the vow I made to our gracious Lord?"

David must have been proud of Absalom's devotion to the Lord. He was certainly grateful to have his son in his presence once again. There was no reason to refuse Absalom's humble request. Hebron was the city that first crowned David as king. He was confident the elders there would also welcome his son. David had no idea of just how welcome in Hebron Absalom would be.

Absalom offered no sacrifices to God. He fulfilled no vows except for a bitter vow to take vengeance on his own father. When the crown prince arrived in Hebron, he quickly spread word that a rebellion against the king had begun. The prince of darkness whom everyone had come to love in these last few years was now ready to steal the throne from his own aging father. Many rallied to Absalom's side—so many in fact that he soon had a larger army in Hebron than David had in Jerusalem.

Far too late, David became aware of his son's rebellion. The humiliated king made the painful decision to evacuate Jerusalem before Absalom arrived to take it by force. David did not want to see the capital destroyed by a civil war. David loved Jerusalem. Furthermore, he knew Absalom had the greater army. His only hope was to retreat back into the Judean wilderness.

This must have been horribly humiliating for David the Great. His own son fomented a rebellion by turning many of his chief leaders, counselors, and greatest warriors against him. The king and the remnant of his army had to slink out of town like frightened dogs. As they sadly left the city, a man named Shimei, a member of Saul's family, cursed David and threw stones at the heartbroken king.

Abishai, never reluctant to kill an idiot, asked permission to take off Shimei's head.

Ever unpredictable, David refused to let anyone kill the man. "My own son wishes to kill me; why shouldn't this relative of Saul?" David explained to the loyal soldiers by his side. "Don't kill him. Don't even stop him from throwing rocks. Maybe he's speaking for God. Maybe not. We don't know yet. We can always kill him later after we learn what God is doing in all this."

With that, the aging king returned to the wilderness of his youth, where he would wait once again for a hateful enemy to hunt him down.

Leadership Focus: Pay attention when you sense a situation is not right.

> *The forensic question is this: Could the disaster have been averted? Amnon had raped Tamar. Absalom murdered Amnon and hated David for never punishing Amnon. Absalom's boiling hatred for his father led to a rebellion many years later that drove David out of his kingdom and put a petty, vengeful tyrant on Israel's throne. Could all this have been prevented?*

David must have sensed something was off when the "sick" Amnon requested that his beautiful sister Tamar cook for him by his bedside and hand-feed him a meal. He should have denied such a request, but instead he blinked. He refused to pay attention to his own inner voice.

Pay attention to your discernment. Listen to the Holy Spirit speaking to your heart. When you feel a situation is not right, when you have that intuitive sense that something is off, take notice. Question the situation. Seek wise counsel. Most importantly, go to God with your concerns. Ask Him if what you're feeling is from Him or if it's just the jitters.

When you sense something is wrong, tap the brakes. Surely in thinking back on this, David must have wished he had paid attention. Hearing Amnon's odd request regarding Tamar, David ignored that check, that inner voice, and a nightmare was the result. His daughter was raped, one son was murdered, and yet another son was leading a rebellion.

Great leaders heed their own inner voice. Three thousand years ago a great king didn't, and a great tragedy befell an entire nation.

Chapter 13

A YOUNG MAN'S GAME

Based on 2 Samuel 16–19

Life on the run, life in the wilderness, is a young man's
game, and as a young man David played it as well as it
can be played. His private army grew as did his legend, and he
became the most famous man in the land.

A generation later, however, the situation was far different.
No longer a young warrior but rather an aging king, David
was again a fugitive in the unforgiving desert. This time it was
because his own son had led a rebellion and driven him out of
Jerusalem.

How humiliating for a king! How utterly shameful for a
father! David had conquered Israel's greatest enemies and made
allies out of other lesser foes. Yet he could not stop his own son
from leading a mutiny against him.

Hiding in the desert for the second time in his life, David
the psalmist immortalized what God was teaching him in this
valley of his life:

> O Lord, I have so many enemies; so many are against me.
> So many are saying, "God will never rescue him!"
>
> But you, O Lord, are a shield around me; you are my
> glory, the one who holds my head high. I cried out to the
> Lord, and he answered me from his holy mountain.
>
> I lay down and slept, yet I woke up in safety, for the
> Lord was watching over me. I am not afraid of ten thou-
> sand enemies who surround me on every side.
>
> Arise, O Lord! Rescue me, my God! Slap all my ene-
> mies in the face! Shatter the teeth of the wicked! Victory
> comes from you, O Lord. May you bless your people.
>
> —Psalm 3

ON THE RUN AGAIN

When King David first sat on the throne in the new capital of Jerusalem, his inaugural act was to send for God's holy ark of the covenant to be brought into the city. David believed that with it would come God's overflowing blessings. Years later, poisoned with bitterness after the rape of his sister, the first act of the self-appointed King Absalom was despicable.

Not knowing if he would ever return to Jerusalem, David left behind ten of his concubines to keep the palace in order. Concubines were not exactly wives, but they were still an official and respectable part of the family. When Absalom learned of the women his father had left behind, he set up a tent on the palace rooftop and one by one raped each of David's concubines in sight of the entire city. He intended to completely humiliate his father and send the message to any David loyalists remaining in Jerusalem that he and his father would never be reconciled and that Absalom was their new king. Beyond that, it was a hideous act of vengeance for the rape of his sister Tamar.

LESSON FROM OLD DR. MARK

Unforgiveness does not hurt the person you refuse to forgive. Unforgiveness in your life poisons only you. Absalom's hatred took root after Amnon's rape of Tamar. After David failed to punish Amnon, Absalom's hatred turned to psychotic poison until Absalom became what he hated—a rapist. If you refuse to let go of your wounds, they will eventually devastate marriages, destroy homes, ruin ministries, and bring companies to destruction. Instead, receive the healing power of God and walk in His forgiveness.

Though David had vacated Jerusalem and left the palace's front doors wide open for Absalom, he was not quite ready for the cemetery or even an early retirement. There were several reasons he left Jerusalem. First, David had never defended a city. He had been an attacker all his life, always on the offense. Of all the military strategies David excelled at, defensive siege warfare was not one of them. He decided it was in his best interest to flee Jerusalem before Absalom even arrived. It would give him time to regroup. He would live to fight another day. Second, the Judean desert was David's secret weapon. Third, he did not want Jerusalem destroyed.

David was experienced enough to know that even a setback such as this one did not mean ultimate defeat. Fleeing Jerusalem was not the end of him. A bend in the road is not the end of the road unless you fail to make the turn, and David would not make that mistake. He had suffered a horrible and humiliating setback, but he would not be defeated.

Rested, regrouped, and restored by God, he planned his attack. He decided to use the same tactic that had taken down Goliath. David would lure the stronger, heavily favored Absalom into the wilderness. That gave the advantage to David's smaller but lethal guerrilla army.

He divided his army into three groups, each with its own general. One was led by Joab, another by Joab's brother Abishai, and a third by Ittai the Gittite. David intended to go into battle with them, but he was quickly talked out of it. "Absalom really only wants to kill you," his men told him. "If he does it would be the same as killing ten thousand of us. Please, my lord, do not give him that opportunity. We are willing to fight our Hebrew brothers for one reason only: to restore you to the throne. If you died today, then all this bloodshed would be in vain."

David wisely submitted to his generals' wisdom and dispatched the three divisions into the forest of Ephraim. He did, however, give them one standing order: "Don't kill my son."

How confusing that command must have been to those willing to give up their lives to place David back on the throne. There was no restoring Absalom. He was way past repentance. That was finished. Absalom had engaged in a horrible deception for years with an aim to forge a rebellion against his father. He humiliated David by capturing the capital city and then raping ten of David's concubines. Clearly Absalom had gone over the edge, yet David commanded his army to not kill him.

LESSON FROM OLD DR. MARK

Watch out for your blind spot. No matter how great a leader you may be, no matter what wonderful vision, creativity, and ability you may have, there is always a blind spot that your enemy will exploit if he can. For David, it was his son. David refused to admit who Absalom had become.

Just as the king had done as a boy facing the giant, his outnumbered army would wait for the arrogant Absalom to bring the battle to them. Once again David proved to be a master strategist. Absalom had a larger, heavier, more cumbersome army, poorly prepared for desert warfare. He also controlled the capital. A wiser military officer with these advantages would not have led his army into a wilderness to face an army of guerillas for whom the desert was a second home. Absalom was so desperate to defeat David that he lost all reason. David's three divisions encircled and outflanked Absalom's army. As 2 Samuel 18 describes it, "There was a great slaughter that day, and twenty thousand men laid down their lives. The battle raged all across the countryside, and more men died because of the forest than were killed by the sword" (vv. 7–8).

David had tempted Absalom's gigantic army into such disadvantageous terrain that soldiers actually stumbled into crevices and fell over cliffs. There was mercy in this for David's troops. Remember that this enemy was not twenty thousand Philistines or Amalekites. They were fellow Jews. David's plan to lure them into difficult terrain meant that more than half of the deaths were a result of the rugged landscape rather than the sword of their Hebrew brothers.

As David had requested, his army did not intentionally try to bring harm to Absalom. However, at one point in the battle after the outcome had become clear, young Absalom was attempting to escape when one of the more ironic scenes in the Bible occurred.

Absalom, who was described as the perfect specimen of a man, cut his hair only once a year and then only because it was too heavy to carry around. Now, trying to escape the battle by fleeing as fast as he could on a mule, Absalom's gorgeous, flowing hair became snagged in the crevice of a large oak tree as he passed under it. His mule kept going, leaving Absalom dangling from the tree by the hair that he was too vain to cut.

Keeping their word, David's soldiers refrain from killing Absalom. Instead, they inform their commander, Joab.

Joab is dumbfounded: "You mean he's hanging there by his hair, defenseless, and you just left him? He has to die. Now!"

The soldiers remind Joab of David's one request. "You couldn't get me to betray King David's command for a thousand pieces of silver! Remember what David did to those guys who killed King Saul? And King Ishbosheth? We're not going to make the same mistake. No way are we going to disobey David."

Joab understood their reasons and could even respect them for it, but he knew he needed to do what David could not bring himself to do. He ordered his men to show him the dangling pretender. Never squeamish about killing, Joab took three arrows and shot them into Absalom's heart. Then ten soldiers drew their swords and plunged them again and again into the body of the usurper.

VICTORY AND PERSONAL PAIN

Since David heeded his soldiers' insistence that he not go to battle, he had no idea of the outcome. Joab immediately sent a runner to David with word of the day's events. The messenger arrived at David's camp rejoicing, "All is well! The Lord has dealt severely with all those who stood against you!" David's immediate response was, "What about young Absalom? Is he all right?"

LESSON FROM OLD DR. MARK

Parents reading this will know exactly what I'm talking about here. If you do not have children yet, just trust me on this. One day you will understand. Your children never grow up in your eyes. It does not matter what they have done, how they have lived, or how they have wounded you—your babies are still your babies. A parent's desire to pick up their children, hug them tight, and promise them everything will be OK never lessens. To all of Israel, Absalom was a dangerous rebel who deserved to die, but to David, Absalom was the little baby boy who once upon a time slept peacefully in his daddy's arms.

"What about young Absalom?" David asked about his son as though he was an innocent child. The naïve messenger did not pick up on the father's concern for his son, and he proudly announced, "May all of your enemies, both now and in the future, be as that young man is!"

Upon hearing the news of his son's death, David was overwhelmed with grief and burst into tears. News of the king's sorrow spread throughout the army. A wet blanket of gloom smothered the joy of victory.

David's loyal soldiers had stuck with their king when no one else would. While villagers on the roadside threw rocks at David and cursed him, his soldiers loved him and remained true. They risked their lives to restore the rightful king. Now, with victory in hand, David's overwhelming grief made them ashamed. They snuck back into Jerusalem with their tails tucked between their legs when they should have been lauded in a victory parade.

Finally, Joab could take it no more. He speaks to David in a way no one else would ever dare. "Listen," he begins, as he approaches the anguished king. "You are ruining this whole victory. Your faithful soldiers risked their lives. They killed for you. You think you had a rebellion on your hands from Absalom? These men have been loyal to you, have fought for you, and you have done nothing but cover their faces with shame. You have made the victors feel as though they lost. Would you have been happier if we had all died and Absalom had lived?"

David sees his error. "Of course, that would not have made me happier," David admits. "Your victory today probably saved my life and the lives of my wives, concubines, and children. I know it saved my throne."

Still, Joab isn't finished. "Absalom was an unrepentant, vengeful murderer who needed to be killed. You tried exile once. How did that work out? I knew you wouldn't kill him, so I did. It doesn't matter that he was your son; this nation is better off without him. Now if you don't get out on that balcony and wave to the people and turn this day of mourning into a celebration, you're going to lose your troops to the first man who shows them appreciation for their loyal service."

At that, the mourning father recognized Joab's wisdom and walked among his soldiers and people, congratulating everyone on the great victory for Israel. David was reinstated as king of Israel, but his personal pain was unfathomable.

Leadership Focus: There will be times when you have to deal with your own wounds privately and not bleed on your followers.

Being a leader is lonely. Sometimes isolation is the only way to handle the burdens of leadership. There will be times when life forces you to go into your room, fall on your face, and pour out your grief before God alone. Then the moment will come when you have to get up, wash your face, walk back into the world, and be the leader your people need. This truth is not going to sit well with some. Hear this though: if you are going to be a hesitant leader, better you never put on the badge.

It is often said that people want to see transparency in their leadership, but transparency is infinitely overrated. I'm not talking about being phony or a hypocrite. I'm simply saying you need to deal with your own private pain yourself. Your family may be hurting, you may be wounded, your heart may be crying out, yet there must be times when you walk among the people and minister to those under your authority. There will be times when even though you can hardly stand up straight, you walk out there and say everything is going to be OK.

David lost his son, a terrible loss for anyone. Yet his soldiers risked their lives and shed blood to place God's anointed king back on the throne. Jerusalem remained intact due to David's wise decision to leave town. Israel was once again under the leadership of the greatest king it would ever know. There was infinite reason to rejoice and celebrate, but David temporarily brought shame on everyone by publicly mourning the loss of a murderer and rapist.

Despite your personal pain, you must (more quickly than you would probably like) come to the point where you can deal with your own grief privately while you show others gratitude. Great leaders know when to walk out on the balcony, wave like the pope, and say, "Thank you very much for your help, encouragement, and strength."

You cannot bleed on your flock if you want them to have confidence in your leadership.

CHAPTER 14

A MOUNTAINTOP GALLOWS

Based on 2 Samuel 20–21

A N INSIDIOUS INDIRECT effect of rebellion is that even if the rebellion fails, confidence in leadership is shaken. Rebellions plant fear and questions in the hearts and minds of many who took no part in the rebellion. "If he doesn't want to put up with the boss, maybe I shouldn't." "If the president gives in to her demands, maybe he'll do the same for me." "If the king's own son didn't believe in his father, maybe the king should be king no longer."

Absalom's rebellion died a swift death, as did Absalom himself, but the lies David's enemy spread throughout Israel lived on. For years the crown prince had spread doubt and discontent. "Too bad my father is too busy to hear your story, because I'd rule in your favor for sure." Demagoguery poisons minds and encourages rebellion. Inevitably some hearts turned against David—hearts he had tried to lead with mercy, wisdom, and grace.

SHEBA

As David was resettling back into Jerusalem, some of those poisoned, bitter minds continued believing Absalom's lies. One such stubborn rebel was a Benjamite named Sheba. This Sheba resented that a Judean king from Bethlehem occupied the throne instead of his fellow Benjamite Saul. He was also bitter that David had moved the capital out of Gibeah to Jerusalem. Convinced that David only cared about Judah, Sheba spread the word among the other tribes, "David is a Judean. All the leaders around him are Judeans. All the generals are Judeans. The priests too. Couldn't he at least have left the capital in Gibeah? This guy isn't the king of all Israel; he only cares about Judah! We don't need him!"

David was barely home in Jerusalem when yet another rebellion and civil war had begun. Sheba had been able to convince Israelites from outside the tribe of Judah to join him in this revolt. Sheba's army, such as it was, encamped in a fortified city and braced for war.

King David still had two armies devoted to him. One was his own private army, led by Joab. These veterans had fought for David and Joab for thirty years ever since organizing in the caves of Adullam. David also had the newer, less experienced Judean army. The general of this army was Amasa. Knowing he would need every available soldier to fight this second rebellion, David sent Amasa to organize his troops. "You have three days, Amasa, to gather them and meet Joab and his army," the king instructed.

Whether he walked when he should have run, or his soldiers were slow to get organized, or if it was a subtle statement of rebellion, Amasa was late to the rendezvous with Joab. Joab, never one to be taken lightly, decided to make it clear to everyone: when the king says three days, he means three days—no exceptions.

Joab approached his fellow general and feigned excitement over the reunion. "Amasa, my brother, how are you doing?" When the general leaned over to hug his brother-in-arms, Joab grabbed Amasa's beard with his right hand to give the impression that he was bringing him in to greet him with a kiss, but in his left hand he held a dagger with which he opened Amasa up. The Bible describes the scene graphically: "his insides gushed out onto the ground" (2 Sam. 20:10). Lovely. Even then Joab refused to finish him off, letting Amasa instead lay on the ground bleeding to death in front of both Joab's and Amasa's armies.

All because he was late to a meeting.

Amasa's writhing body made Joab's point clear. Obey the king's orders. Anything less means death.

Joab said absolutely nothing. Why would he? His actions spoke loudly enough. Instead, he rather coolly got back on his horse and headed in the direction of Sheba. As the troops were still making sense out of what just happened, one of Joab's young officers pulled Amasa's body to the side of the road and said, "If you're with Joab, follow us."

No surprise, they all went with Joab. Immediately.

LESSON FROM OLD DR. MARK

When the king, or the boss, or someone else God has placed in authority over you says three days, he means three days—seventy-two hours, not ninety-six or even seventy-five. If you are told to report at 8:00, get there at 7:55, not 8:05. Learn from Amasa's mistake.

Punctuality may, at first glance, seem an archaic virtue in the information age. In fact, it is becoming more important, not less. In the not so distant past, the truism of business was that "the big eat the small." Not anymore. Now the fast eat the slow.

In a world where speed is victory, time is money. Show up late to meet me and you make a clear statement that my time is worth less than yours. No one wants to do business on that basis. While you shilly-shally, while you dither and procrastinate, some bright kid has pressed "send" and it's too late. Be there. Be there ready. Be there prepared and in possession of the facts and armed for battle.

However, this story is not just about punctuality. It is about the appearance of evil. Amasa had joined one rebellion: Absalom's. Remarkably, Amasa had lived through that. Forgiven by David, he had been welcomed back into the fold and even restored to a position of great responsibility.

If ever he needed to show he respected David's authority, if ever he needed desperately to demonstrate loyalty and full dedication to David's kingdom, surely it was in the face of this new rebellion by Sheba. By being late to the rendezvous, he gave his enemies plenty of reason to doubt both his loyalty and his leadership.

Not everyone is going to immediately discern how wonderful, loyal, effective, and virtuous you are. You may just have a few along the way that need to be won over. Don't give them proof that their doubts about you are justified. Show up unprepared, be late with your work, or give it less than your best, and you may learn the hard way what David's son Solomon meant when he wrote, "The soul of the sluggard craves and gets nothing, while the soul of the diligent is richly supplied" (Prov. 13:4, ESV).

When Joab and his now unified army found Sheba inside the fortified city of Abel-beth-maacah, the rebellion was suppressed as easily as Joab could have hoped. The hard work was done by an influential woman in the city. She convinced the right people that justice, and safety for that matter, lay with David and Joab, not Sheba. Moments later, she tossed Sheba's head over the wall to Joab. And that was that. Rebellion over.

With this good news reported back to David, the king must have said to himself, "Now, at last, surely I will finally have that season of peace I've been waiting for."

Not. So. Fast.

THE FAMINE

Second Samuel 21 begins, "There was a famine during David's reign that lasted for three years, so David asked the LORD about it. And the LORD said, 'The famine has come because Saul and his family are guilty of murdering the Gibeonites'" (v. 1).

In Joshua 9 the Gibeonites had tricked the invading Israelites into sparing their lives, an arrangement Joshua and the other leaders had ratified with an oath. Even though the Gibeonites had achieved their survival through somewhat devious means, God takes oaths seriously. Saul broke that oath and killed some Gibeonites. Decades later all of Israel was suffering from a famine because of their previous king's sin.

LESSON FROM OLD DR. MARK

This story of the famine and the Gibeonites is old covenant theology and difficult for us to wrap our minds around. God dealt with it later in Jeremiah 31:30 when He said, "All people will die for their own sins—those who eat the sour grapes will be the ones whose mouths will pucker." Yet there is still a way for unrepented, unresolved evil to come back to you. Anything you can set right, set it right. Anything you can pay back, pay it back. Anybody you can apologize to, do not hesitate. Settle things. Pay your bills. Do not let negative things float around loose in the universe. They are bound to come right back and hit you in the head

God did not tell David what needed to be done to make restitution. Instead, the wise king went to the Gibeonites himself and asked, "How can we make things right with you for Saul breaking his oath and killing some of your ancestors all those years ago?"

They told David, "Money won't do it. Instead, we need seven descendants of Saul brought to us so that we may execute them ourselves. This will pay the debt Israel owes us."

David understood the law. He understood oaths and debt and retribution. He held in high regard the expectations placed on the children of Israel. This request by the Gibeonites made sense to David, and he knew better than to refuse or even to negotiate a lesser punishment.

Years before, David had made a vow with his friend Jonathan, Saul's son, to always protect each other as well as each other's children. After Jonathan's death, the young king of Israel honored that covenant by inviting Jonathan's crippled son Mephibosheth to live with him as family. There was no way David was going to make restitution for one broken vow by breaking another, so Mephibosheth was not offered as a sacrifice. Instead, he brought to the Gibeonites five grandsons of Saul, and two of his surviving sons, whose mother was Saul's concubine Rizpah.

The Gibeonites accepted David's offering and hanged the seven men on the mountain as the barley harvest began. Interestingly, the Scriptures are clear about when God ended the famine, and it was not at the final breaths of the seven executed men. One might think that the famine would have come to an immediate end, even as the raging storm calmed when those sailors threw Jonah into the sea (Jonah 1:15). This was not the case, however. Instead, God had plans for one more beautiful story.

Rizpah knew she was powerless to prevent the deaths of her two sons. All she could do, she did. Day after day, night after night, the grieving mother faithfully guarded her sons' bodies. During the day she kept vultures from tearing their bodies, and at night she slept with one eye open so that she could drive away wild animals. She refused to give up on her sons. She did not care what anybody thought, nor did she allow the sight and smell of the rotting corpses to keep her from protecting the bodies of the boys she loved.

LESSON FROM OLD DR. MARK

Rizpah's love for her boys, her vigilant faith even beyond death, is as powerful a picture of diligent, prayerful intercession as there is in the Bible. It is a brutal and awkward story to preach from. It is a rare preacher who is willing to lift up the complicated common-law wife of an evil king to illustrate what a faithful, prayerful mother looks like. It is nonetheless true that Rizpah absolutely refused to give up on her children. Her selfless dedication is a model for modern parents.

When David learned of Rizpah's months-long intercession for her sons, he gathered up the bones of Saul and Jonathan that the people of Jabesh-gilead had retrieved after their deaths, as well as the bodies of the two sons of Rizpah, and buried them all together in the tomb of Saul's father in the Benjamite town of Zela. "After that," the Scriptures tell us, "God ended the famine in the land" (2 Sam. 21:14).

Restitution for Saul's sin had been paid, and the intercession of a vigilant mother had led to an honorable burial of a concubine's sons in the same tomb as the first king of Israel.

Now. No more rebellion. Right? No more famine. Right? Finally, David could put his feet up in his last years—right?

Of course not. Enter the Philistines...again. The Philistines hated David personally even more than they hated Israel.

Perhaps now, they reasoned, the aging king would be easier pickings.

Initially, the gray-haired David tried reliving the warrior days of his youth when he so utterly dominated the Philistines. However, after a close call with a son of Goliath, another giant named Ishbi-benob, David's soldiers pleaded with their king, "Please let us handle this war! If they kill you, that's the end of us." The wise king submitted and allowed the younger soldiers to fight his war.

LESSON FROM OLD DR. MARK

There comes a time when generals have to stay on the hill and watch through the field glasses. Everybody likes the romantic idea of a general leading his army into battle, but the moment will come when it is simply best to send the young boys out to fight. An American Air Force officer once told me that there comes a time when you have to quit flying and start training pilots.

Only after David relented and returned to camp did he discover just how many giant slayers he had inspired. Previously, Abishai had killed the giant who cornered David. Later, in the town of Gob, Sibbecai killed another son of Goliath named Saph, and Elhanan brought down Goliath's brother. When the battle moved to the Philistine capital of Gath, David's nephew Jonathan toppled yet another giant son of Goliath who had twelve fingers and twelve toes. David slew one giant. His influence on a generation made others into giant-killers.

With the giants slain and the Philistines conquered yet again, David and the Israelites returned to Israel. This campaign against the Philistines, incidentally, is what ultimately broke the back of the Philistine domination in the Middle East.

Eventually the pagan cultures of the Edomites, Amalekites, Amorites, Hittites, and Philistines blended into a thoroughly beaten and subdued group that together assumed the name of "Philistines." They were never again a serious military threat.

Leadership Focus: The enemy may have more giants than you know. You do not have to kill them all yourself.

The apostle Peter warned us, "Watch out for your great enemy, the devil. He prowls around like a roaring lion, looking for someone to devour" (1 Pet. 5:8). This lion, this enemy of our souls, is relentless. He will never give up trying to bring us down.

Just when David thought he had seen the last of the Philistines, they attacked again. When he thought he had long ago faced and defeated the biggest giant of his life, more giants attacked.

The youthful David was virile enough to bring down Goliath, as well as countless other Philistines in his early days of battle. The aging David needed younger soldiers to kill new giants.

If you have spent your life in leadership gathering to you those willing to rally to your cause, you do not have to kill every giant yourself. God will bring to you those people who will strengthen your hand and be a vital part of your leadership team. Shower them with praise. Teach them. Train them. Discipline them. Sooner or later, however, you must allow them to find their own strength. Let them find their own place in battle.

Never let yourself yield to envy for the young giant killers you've trained. That was Saul's disorder.

Instead, be thankful for them. The enemy may have more giants than you are aware of. The day will come when you cannot kill them all alone.

Remember too that in the same way that the leader gets the blame when things go wrong, when everything goes right the one in leadership gets the credit. David did not kill even one of those four final Philistine giants. In fact, he was not even on the battlefield for three of their deaths. However, 2 Samuel 21 ends with, "David and his warriors killed [the giants]" (v. 22).

When in leadership, share the load and share the credit. Then do not worry. God will shine plenty of light on you.

David, CEO

In all that has been taught and written about David, his considerable management skills are seldom mentioned. From a militia of farm boys and six hundred grim guerillas he forged a phenomenally successful national army, and he made a nation out of disparate and sometimes warring tribes.

First Chronicles 22–29 gives us a look at David the Great, CEO. Nearing the end of an astonishing career, at a time when many executives are ready to hang up their cleats and spend their last few years in leisure, David prepares the nation for his own passing.

These chapters, while they make for some pretty tedious reading, show an executive David selflessly dedicating his rapidly fading strength to the transition ahead.

He prepared for the construction of the temple.

Though God has not allowed him to build it himself, he assembled the necessary material for construction. He carefully went over the blueprints with Solomon in great detail and surrendered the project and all the vast material he had accumulated. Surely he knew that neither history nor the Bible would give him credit. The temple would never be called David's Temple. It was to be Solomon's Temple and David knew that.

He also demonstrated his remarkable fundraising ability.

He raised a phenomenal amount for the temple with astonishingly modern professionalism. First of all he gave a clear inventory of what the government had already purchased.

It is easier to raise money if you're not starting from scratch. He listed gold, silver, bronze, iron, precious stones of all kinds, and marble, which he had assembled with state funds.

Then he led the way with personal generosity. May I say, incredible generosity. He announced he was giving three thousand talents of gold and seven thousand talents of refined silver. Those who claim to know such things say that this amounted to about ten billion dollars. I will leave the arithmetic to others. What I will say is this. It could have been a great deal less than ten billion and still have been a fortune that David gave personally.

Next he called on the leaders to lead. His own generosity set the pace and they stepped up to the plate, big time. Thousands of talents.

Finally, he went to the people.

Seeing that the government, the king, and the leaders had done their part, the people gave "willingly and with great joy." One estimation puts the total cost of the temple at fifty-six billion dollars. That's what I call a capital campaign!

He carefully restructured the artistic, religious, and financial communities.

He established the organization of musicians (never easy to organize), the priests, and even the gatekeepers. He also set accountants in place for the national treasure and set up managers for state-run businesses. He made sure that capable overseers were in place to run the nation's considerable agricultural businesses. He even restructured the tribal councils. Last of all he set up a cabinet, an advisory council, and national security teams to assist his successor.

None of this is as exciting as slaying giants or defeating vast Philistine armies, but it reveals an underreported and undervalued aspect of David's genius. David the Great was not just a charismatic visionary. He was a manager par excellence.

CHAPTER 15

THE HALL OF FAME

Based on 2 Samuel 23

To SEE THE real King David, to see his intricate inner working, his ups and downs, and his deep psychological complexities, is to see a man who will not fit on a Sunday school felt board. It is furthermore to ask, "What is the deal with David?"

The question remains to be answered. "How can David be called a man after God's own heart?" He had blood up to his elbows. He killed thousands of people—not all in combat. He once brought devastation upon his nation. He was not good at marriage. He raised his children poorly, and he committed both adultery and murder.

Yet somehow at the end of this complicated life, there remained in David a fixation on the Lord. David never lied to God, to himself, or to his nation about who he was. He confessed in prayer, on paper, and in public that he was a mixed bag. David was not perfect, and he wanted this remembered for all time. Instead, the God he served was the perfect One, and David published that whenever he had an opportunity. He said, "When I was unfaithful to God, He was faithful to me. When I couldn't raise my own kids right, He raised me right. The Lord has steadfastly remained a shield and refuge for me, and my heart remains fixed on Him."

In David's final years, his sword was retired and his bold strides became the slow and cautious steps of the elderly. He seldom strolled his rooftop in the evenings. Instead, he spent his late-night hours with his transition team and transcribers documenting the final words and wishes of Israel's greatest king. The mixed legacy of David the Great would continue to impact lives throughout history by pointing others not toward his complicated seventy years but toward the God who anointed a child as king.

LAST WORDS

"These are the last words of David," begins 2 Samuel 23:1. However, that does not mean these were the final words he spoke before he took his last breath. It rather means that David, having recognized he was nearing the end of his life, had called to his side a historian and wished to compose a summation, a last will and testament of sorts. Nothing was being bequeathed exactly. It was the final memoir of a king determined for all to know the truth. It is no surprise that even at the end of his life, David began this summation in song:

> David, the son of Jesse, speaks—David, the man who was raised up so high, David, the man anointed by the God of Jacob, David, the sweet psalmist of Israel.
>
> The Spirit of the LORD speaks through me; his words are upon my tongue. The God of Israel spoke. The Rock of Israel said to me: "The one who rules righteously, who rules in the fear of God, is like the light of morning at sunrise, like a morning without clouds, like the gleaming of the sun on new grass after rain."
>
> Is it not my family God has chosen? Yes, he has made an everlasting covenant with me. His agreement is arranged and guaranteed in every detail. He will ensure my safety and success. But the godless are like thorns to be thrown away, for they tear the hand that touches them. One must use iron tools to chop them down; they will be totally consumed by fire.
>
> —2 SAMUEL 23:1–7

Despite all that he had accomplished for Israel during his reign, David refused to steal the glory for himself. For David, it had all been about God, which we see in his words: "David, the man who was raised up so high...the man anointed by the God of Jacob....The Spirit of the LORD speaks through me" (vv. 1–2).

It was God who killed the lion, the bear, and Goliath. It was God who kept David safe all those years on the run from Saul. It was God who strengthened and expanded Israel beyond anyone's imagination as the young nation all but annihilated the once overpowering Philistines. In this final summation, David was more than clear: the glory for all of Israel's success was to be given to God.

The King James Version translates verse 5 as: "Although my house be not so with God; yet he hath made with me an everlasting covenant." In other words, "Even though my house is not with God as it ought to be, God has never broken His covenant with me." Plain and simple, David did a better job leading his country than he did his household, and he did not deny that.

In 2 Samuel 7, even as God forbade David to build Him a temple, the Lord established a covenant with David: "Your house and your kingdom will continue before me for all time, and your throne will be secure forever" (v. 16). After this covenant was established, David began to damage the earthly family God had given him through his adultery with Bathsheba, his refusal to discipline Amnon, and the rebellion of Absalom. Regardless of David's failures, God remained true to His covenant with David. David the psalmist lifted up the Lord's unfailing faithfulness even from his deathbed.

LESSON FROM OLD DR. MARK

How can we connect all this with 1 Timothy 3:5? Despite the king's gigantic blunders within his own family, why did God pick David? Concerning those aspiring to become church leaders, Paul wrote: "For if a man cannot manage his own household, how can he take care of God's church?"

Paul makes a great point to be sure. Of course a man should have authority in his own house and do all that he can to manage his own family. However, verses such as 1 Timothy 3:5, when they are mashed up against the single flat horizon of legalism, become not more but less true and less helpful in the face of life's complications.

It is true that leaders ought to be the best leaders they can be in their own homes. Still, their followers don't have permission to work backward from the leader's children's sins to invalidate their leadership.

God raised Adam. He taught Adam, instructed him, and made the rules clear to him. God and Adam walked side by side in the garden. Yet Adam sinned. He disobeyed his heavenly Father. Does that invalidate God's leadership in the universe?

Though two loving parents may do absolutely everything right in raising their family under God's direction, their children still have a God-given, inalienable right to their own sins. Having said all that, David admitted in 2 Samuel 23 that he did not do everything right, yet God remained true to him.

What are we left with? A merciful and gracious God who remembers His word. To God be the glory!

Only after giving all the glory to God, David began lifting up his loyal soldiers, to give them their well-deserved share in the glory of Israel's successes. An honorable and humble staff will be quick to say, "We are ants. We are nothing, really. Our leader—he's the man. He's the one who should be acknowledged." Likewise, an honorable and humble leader will tell all who will listen, "My team is incredible! I've hired people smarter than I am, better than I am. Look at all they've accomplished. We need to make sure it's their names in the hall of fame, not mine." Knowing he was running out of time to do so, David felt compelled to make sure he shared the glory with his team, some of whom had been with him since the cave at Adullam.

David made a list of thirty-seven men, hall of famers whose loyalty to David had impacted his life and left a mark on history. David began his list by reminiscing about Jashobeam, Eleazar, and Shammah—also known as "The Three," an elite circle at the top of David's mightiest men. David did not want to miss an opportunity to mention some of their greatest feats in battle, including a time when one killed eight hundred enemy warriors in a single battle with just a spear.

He next shared exploits of Abishai and also Benaiah, who killed a lion in a pit on a snowy day. His age and hard life catching up to him, David was eager to get these stories recorded. These great men were a part of his story, and David did not want them forgotten.

HONORING URIAH

At some point during this storytelling session with a historian, it is possible that the tired, aging David asked for others to help simply jot down the names of all the rest of his mighty men. He wished he could share stories of them all, but at least he would make sure their names were recorded so that three thousand years later people would know who David considered his most faithful men.

We can imagine a scene in which one of his staff members comes to David's bedside and says, "Your Majesty, we have thirty-six men listed here now. Thirty-six incredible soldiers whom we think you would want listed for their commitment to you and to Israel."

The feeble king lifts up his head from the pillow and extends his hand. "Let me see the list. I want to make sure you're not forgetting someone."

As he reads the list of names, smiling as he remembers their faithfulness, David says, "Yes, these are the greatest men I ever worked with. What a team! May their names be remembered forever."

David scans the list one more time and looks up somberly. "There's one name missing."

Everyone around him looks down at their sandal straps, knowing exactly whose name is missing. Finally, somebody works up the nerve to respond, "Your Majesty, we don't have to list him. We really don't. Let's not remind everyone of this part of your life. It was a minor blemish in the corner of an otherwise beautiful canvas."

Immediately, David says to them, "No, he must be added to this list. I was disloyal to him, but he was loyal to me. He never sinned against me; I sinned against him. Add his name to the list. Do it now. And don't even think of hiding it in the middle of all these names. Put his name at the end, where no one can miss it."

Verse 39 lists the thirty-seventh and final loyal man David wanted to make sure the world would never forget: Uriah the Hittite.

For all his wickedness, for all his sins, for all his complicated life, David was never a man to hide from reality. Uriah the Hittite—the steadfast soldier who refused to sleep with his wife while his comrades were sleeping in the mud, the husband of Bathsheba, the woman with whom David committed adultery; this same Uriah the Hittite was one of David's mightiest men. Just the name alone was a sober reminder of the dark, scandalous time in the godly king's life. David had repented, everyone had moved on, and Bathsheba's son Solomon was even in line as the next king. Who would have blamed David for leaving Uriah's name off of the list? Yet David did not leave him off. That is David at his best.

This is the complexity of David the Great. He did not want his sins hidden in the pages of history if it meant hiding the loyalty of others or the grace of God. Even at the end of his life, David's heart remained focused on God. He refused to lie about who he was. He said, "I'm a mixed bag. I admit it. I have messed up in ways I would've thought unimaginable. I couldn't even raise my own household correctly or refrain from murdering one of my best friends. I want it all written down. I want it remembered that though I was not loyal to Uriah, he was loyal to me. Though I was unfaithful to God, God remained faithful to me."

At the end of the life of the greatest king in Israel's history, with all the triumphant notches on his belt of victories and accomplishments, David simply said, "Who God is, is more important than who I am. Let all my sins be known so that God's grace will never be forgotten."

Leadership Focus: The wise leader knows he cannot win his battles alone.

David's entire life was anointed by the supernatural power of God. From learning to play the lyre alone in the wilderness to listening for the wind in the mulberry trees before attacking the Philistines, the hand of God led every step of David's life and guided him from victory to victory. Second Samuel 22 is David's reflection on all the incredible work God chose to do through the shepherd king: "In your strength, I can crush an army; with my God I can scale any wall.... You have armed me with strength for the battle; you have subdued my enemies under my feet. You placed my foot on their necks.... You gave me victory over my accusers" (vv. 30, 40–41, 44).

Throughout the psalm, and throughout his life, David's theme was "God, God, God," not "me, me, me." David was clear about what was his and what was God's. His sins were on him; his victories were on God. David never denied that, and neither should we. In Isaiah 42:8, God said, "I am the LORD; that is my name! I will not give my glory to anyone else." If like Saul, a leader becomes too full of himself, God can raise up a shepherd boy to take his place.

Like David, great leaders give God the glory. They also generously acknowledge the great men and women who have shared the miles and the battles. Great leaders make sure those people are recognized for their work. The great Israelite king of forty years who had brought down giants and vanquished nations made sure he listed the names of soldiers who helped him do so.

It was David whom these soldiers loved, to whom they were loyal, and of whom they were in awe. David, however, said, "No, it wasn't me. Not in the least. First of all, it was God who gave us victory after victory. Secondly, these are the men who devoted themselves to me in ways I never dared ask, even when it meant sleeping in caves and hiding from Saul. If not for them, I would've spent the rest of my life like a hermit in Adullam. These amazing men believed in me and encouraged me to find strength in the Lord and receive all that God had for me."

A wise leader will always keep at the forefront of his mind that whatever he has accomplished, he has done so by God's grace. Nor has he achieved his victories without the loyal men and women whom God placed around him.

CHAPTER 16

STRANGE BEDFELLOWS

Based on 1 Kings 1

I N A SENSE, as I've already said, David's childhood was taken by God. When he was a shepherd too young to join the army, God used David to turn the tide of the war against the Philistines and made him a national celebrity. While David was hiding in the wilderness, God used the desert time to build up David's army and weaken Israel's enemies.

At the end of his life, this high-impact leader could not even die in peace. While David lay on his deathbed, a byzantine plot was churning to frustrate David's will and hijack his inheritance. In the face of this plot, politics did indeed make strange bedfellows. A long-embittered ally would finally show his true colors, a power-hungry general would turn out to be loyal only to himself, and a prophet would make sure the son of an adulteress became the next king.

This Machiavellian political intrigue swirled around David in his final days.

David, the Lion of Judah, was now an old man unable to keep warm.

THE AILING KING

David had been king for almost forty years, thirty-three of them over all of Israel. In today's terms that is ten four-year US presidential terms, at least five different sitting presidents. For four decades David had been Israel's principal military, political, and religious leader. There was a high priest, as well as prophets, but it was David who brought the ark to Jerusalem. It was David's songs the people sang when they worshipped. While not a priest, David was certainly at the center of Israel's religious culture.

David established the capital city of Jerusalem, having taken it from the Jebusites. Everywhere people turned in the capital, people were reminded of David. For forty years he had been their leader in every way. Israel was David, and David was Israel.

Now in his seventieth year, David and all of Israel knew that the future of the nation without David's leadership had to be dealt with. David, never given to denial, faced his poor health and age with characteristic honesty. His servants found a young girl, Abishag, to lie next to the king to keep his chilled bones warm. Feeble, stricken with bad circulation, and nearing death, the king was confined to bed while nefarious plots surfaced among those not dreading, but eagerly awaiting an Israel without David.

LESSON FROM OLD DR. MARK

One of the most complicated and dangerous times in the life of any church is when the pastor resigns or dies. There's always someone on the board or in some position of influence who has had a gripe with the pastor, and now he will take this opportunity to step in and get his way. A church that has had solid pastoral leadership for twenty years can blow up in pieces during the transition, when egos are larger than hearts for ministry. The same problem haunts businesses and nations. At the moment of leadership transition, bad character, perhaps hidden for years, can surface with devastating results.

ADONIJAH'S PLOT

At David's impending death, David's son Adonijah, whose mother was Haggith, decided on his own that he would be the next king. The Scriptures say that Adonijah "provided himself with chariots and charioteers and recruited fifty men to run in front of him" (1 Kings 1:5).

Does that sound familiar? Another son of David, aspiring to assume the throne obtained chariots, horses, and soldiers, and galloped through city as though he were already king. That other son of course was Absalom, just before he gathered up his rebellious army. Years later, despite the way it turned out for the vain Absalom, Adonijah tried the same vainglorious tactic. Apparently he learned nothing from his elder brother's disastrous attempt to become king. Surely he had heard the story of Absalom's body hanging from a tree limb with a fist full of arrows through his heart. Surely. Yet the lesson was lost on Adonijah.

David also, it seems, had learned little from his previous mistakes with his children. Years before, he had failed to discipline Amnon after the rape of his sister. He never dealt properly with Absalom's murder of his brother, and he never brought Adonijah to heel. The Bible says, "Now his father, King David, had never disciplined him at any time, even by asking, 'Why are you doing that?'" (1 Kings 1:6). In other words, David spoiled Adonijah. Israel's great king ran the entire country with supernatural wisdom and strategy, but he could not manage his sons.

It is fascinating to read about the bizarre coalition of forces described in 1 Kings 1:7: "Adonijah took Joab son of Zeruiah and Abiathar the priest into his confidence, and they agreed to help him become king."

Since he copied a page right out of Absalom's playbook on how to present himself as king, Adonijah obviously thought well of his big brother. So why would he seek an alliance with Joab, the man who killed Absalom? The answer? Because he cannot claim the throne if he does not have military power, and he would rather team up with the murderer of his brother than do without power.

That begs another question: Why would Joab go along with this plot? David's nephew had devoted his life to protecting David, to leading his armies, and to disposing of anyone who stood in their way. Now why, at the end of David's life, would Joab switch loyalties from a legendary king to an ambitious and devious lightweight? Once again, it is about power. Joab knew that if he helped make Adonijah the next king, the inexperienced young ruler would have no choice but to keep Joab in charge of the military. In fact, Joab would be even more powerful. He would not only have the army in the palm of his hands, he would also hold the king there as well. It was too much temptation for a man who had spent his life playing second fiddle to a legend.

LESSON FROM OLD DR. MARK

Be very careful of the person who says he can make you king. If he can make you king, he can unmake you as well, and he will remind you of it every day of your life.

In addition to Joab, Adonijah also enlisted the help of Abiathar the priest. The name of Abiathar may not ring a bell immediately, but his story is important. Fleeing from Saul, David received bread and Goliath's sword from Ahimelech, the priest at Nob who was Abiathar's father. When Saul heard of this, he slaughtered them all, including Abiathar's father. Only young Abiathar escaped the massacre and fled to David at Adullam.

For the rest of David's life Abiathar stood by David as his priest. Deep in his heart, however, Abiathar harbored resentment toward David for his father's death. If David had not gone to Nob and lied about being on a special mission for the king, Ahimelech and the rest of the priests at Nob would not have been killed. Abiathar waited, bided his time, and then in David's dying days he exacted his revenge.

LESSON FROM OLD DR. MARK

If one of your subordinates despises you and holds a grudge against you, they may suppress it—for a while. Even if they're not aware that the resentment is still there, in a moment of weakness it can rise up and haunt both you and them.

Adonijah, the arrogant and vain prince; Joab, the ruthless general who killed Absalom; and Abiathar, the son of a priest Saul had killed more than forty years earlier—these were unholy confederates who joined forces to lead one final rebellion. Their plan was to hold a dinner party, omitting from the guest list anyone who might oppose them—especially Solomon, David's son by Bathsheba. David had promised Bathsheba to make Solomon his successor and that made him Adonijah's worst enemy.

The thinking behind the secret plan was based on the idea that possession is nine-tenths of the law. With everyone gathered together, save those who might be loyal to Solomon, David's top general, Joab, would anoint Adonijah the new king and then lead him into the palace to assume the throne. Joab wanted military power, Abiathar wanted revenge and religious power, and together they knew they could make Adonijah their puppet.

Politics makes strange bedfellows indeed. However, God can also forge some interesting alliances. To counterattack this axis of evil, God brought together an equally unlikely team of allies.

NATHAN AND BATHSHEBA

David's choice to succeed him on the throne had already been made in private—Solomon the son of Bathsheba. Yet this decision had not been made public. When Nathan the prophet got wind of Adonijah's dinner party, he knew he had to act fast, and he knew who he needed—Bathsheba.

It is a moment of high drama. Roughly thirty years before, Nathan had walked into the palace, publicly denounced David and Bathsheba's sin of adultery, and announced that the judgment for their sin would be the death of their newborn baby. It is very possible that to Bathsheba, Nathan was the prophet who shamed her publicly and took away her child and that she never wanted to see him again.

Now, thirty years later, the elderly Bathsheba assumed that her other son Solomon would soon be the next king as David had promised. Imagine her horror when Nathan came to see her once again. Her heart must have stopped upon learning the prophet had come again with a word from God.

"My lady," the prophet begins immediately, skipping pleasantries, "a plan is afoot to anoint Adonijah the next king. That plot is underway at this very moment."

Whatever had entered Bathsheba's mind at news of the prophet's visit, she now focuses on one thing only. "But the king has promised the throne to Solomon! And Adonijah knows that! If he is made king, he will kill both me and my son before the sun comes up tomorrow."

Nathan nods. "We cannot let that happen. We need to convince David right now to announce his choice of Solomon as Israel's next king!"

While Joab's motivation for anointing the next king was military and political power, and Abiathar's was religious power, Nathan's motivations for joining forces with a woman who despised and feared him was not about power at all. Nathan wanted the will of God. Nathan had a pure spirit and knew he had to follow God's leading. There was no political or religious power in this for him. He would obey God and then disappear once again.

LESSON FROM OLD DR. MARK

Someone once said to me, "It doesn't seem like the kind of thing that God would do following an adulterous affair and a baby that died as a result of sin, to then make the next child of David and Bathsheba the king of Israel." To me, it seems exactly like the kind of thing a God grace would do. God is the perfect disciplinarian. He knows exactly when to chasten you and exactly when to take you up in His arms and love on you. It is so like God that the one whom He disciplines the hardest is the one He loves the most.

Nathan and Bathsheba carefully formed their plan to convince the king to appoint Solomon to the throne. First, Bathsheba would go to David's bedside to remind him of his promise concerning Solomon and inform him of Adonijah's plot. Then Nathan would enter shortly afterward to confirm the news. They knew that they could not both storm into his bedchambers with this disturbing conspiracy theory or they would risk confusing the feeble king. Instead, they would layer the story, one at a time, hoping David would understand the urgency of the matter and take immediate action.

The moment came. Bathsheba enters the king's bedchambers. She says to her weak, ailing husband, "Your Majesty, you promised me that our son Solomon would be Israel's next king, yet your son Adonijah has gathered Joab, Abiathar, and many others for a party to anoint him as your successor. What can be done about this? If Abiathar becomes king, Solomon will be in the grave rather than on the throne."

Before David can even respond to Bathsheba's alarming news, Nathan arrives as planned and confirms for the king what Bathsheba has just said.

"Sir, are you aware that Adonijah, at this very moment, is hosting a party with Joab, Abiathar, and many others, telling them that he is the next king? Is this of your doing?"

Bathsheba then adds, "Whatever Adonijah is planning only works if you do nothing. All of Israel is looking to you and you alone. Who will be the next king? What will you do?"

LESSON FROM OLD DR. MARK

One of the most difficult parts of leadership is succession. While the leader is young, healthy, and effective, everything is going great. When he begins to stagger and stumble toward the finish line, there has to be a plan of succession. If not, leadership and power are likely to fall into the hands of the most conniving and power hungry.

In 1 Kings 1:29–30, David declared to Bathsheba, "As surely as the LORD lives, who has rescued me from every danger, your son Solomon will be the next king and will sit on my throne this very day, just as I vowed to you before the LORD, the God of Israel."

To the great relief of his wife—who had spent roughly thirty years knowing that everywhere she went people whispered to each other about her adultery—David expanded on his plan. He knew the announcement of Solomon as his successor had to be made with a splash, a huge splash, a real spectacle that would show Adonijah's secret dinner party for what it was.

With the mother of the future king and the prophet Nathan at his bedside, David sends for Zadok the priest and Benaiah, his most trusted advisor.

When all are gathered, the king explains his plan: "Take Solomon and my officials down to Gihon Spring. Solomon is to ride on my own mule. There Zadok the priest and Nathan the prophet are to anoint him king over Israel. Blow the ram's horn and shout, 'Long live King Solomon!' Then escort him back here, and he will sit on my throne. He will succeed me as king, for I have appointed him to be ruler over Israel and Judah" (1 Kings 1:33–35).

David knew what Joab knew: possession is nine-tenths of the law. With Solomon on the king's mule, a shout from a priest announcing Solomon as king, and a prophet overseeing it all, Israel would immediately recognize and honor the anointing of their new king.

While Adonijah and Joab were at their dinner party, the new king was anointed at the spring of Gihon—close enough to the dinner party for the attendees to hear the trumpets blare. Confusion reigned in that party. Questions flew. The answer burst in from the street. God's choice, Solomon, had just assumed the throne.

Leadership Focus: Trust in God's will, even when the Spirit is leading in ways you find completely bizarre.

Imagine a conversation that Nathan might have had with a friend before leaving for the palace the day of Solomon's anointing. "I must help Bathsheba put her son Solomon on the throne."

"You mean the ex-wife of Uriah the Hittite, who slept with the king while her husband was at war, got pregnant, married David after the convenient death of her husband, then had the baby that died shortly after you humiliated her and made their scandal public? You mean that Bathsheba?"

"That's the one."

It must have been hard for Nathan to hear all this from God. Surely it was. Wasn't he human? Why would he want to get tangled up in this again after so long? Because he had a word from God. For Nathan it was that simple and he, being a pure spirit, knew what he had to do despite the risks involved.

God's logic is not our logic. He is not bothered by how the world perceives His acts. The Holy Spirit has a long résumé of leading God's children in unusual ways to accomplish His will, and that list is only getting longer.

Trust in God's leading. Trust in His word to you. Do not concern yourself with trifles such as safety or the opinions others. Whatsoever He saith unto thee, do it.

CHAPTER 17

A DANGEROUS, DYING LION

———

Based on 1 Kings 2

D AVID DESERVED ALL the honors heaped on him in his long, full life. He truly was a master of multiple trades. Shepherd. Musician. Poet. Giant slayer. Warrior. Mercenary. Military strategist. Politician. Spiritual leader. King. Now in the last few moments of his life, David knew he had one more grim task he could not avoid.

Since that day almost sixty years before when the prophet Samuel had stolen his boyhood, Israel was at the forefront of David's mind. Whether he was in Bethlehem, Gibeah, Naioth, Adullam, Gath, Ziklag, Hebron, or Jerusalem, David had been concerned with only two things: serving God and serving Israel.

A "man after God's own heart" does not change or forget his lifelong motivations just because he is drawing his final breaths. The second king of Israel had devoted a lifetime of service to expanding Israel's borders, annihilating its ene-mies, suppressing mutinies, and ensuring God's blessings upon the young nation. Now, as he lay dying, he knew there were enemies—ruthless, powerful enemies—that Solomon had to deal with, and it fell to David to give the orders.

It is hard to listen to David's deathbed hit list. The King of Israel sounds like the dying Don Corleone in *The Godfather*, passing to his son Michael the names of everyone he needed to make disappear. David tells Solomon in no uncertain terms who must be dealt with. David did what he had to, and Solomon was well warned.

Even so, King Solomon's first act as king was to spare the life of his brother Adonijah "if he proves himself to be loyal" (1 Kings 1:52). "Go home and stay out of trouble," the king told his brother. "If I even catch a whiff of anything but complete loyalty to your new king, there will be no more mercy extended your way. You are forever on the shortest of leashes."

Adonijah was given a chance to redeem himself. What follows is the rest of David's list.

JOAB

"Do with him what you think best, but don't let him grow old and go to his grave in peace" (1 Kings 2:6). David's instructions to Solomon regarding his top general and nephew were both open and clear. "Use your discretion and great wisdom to determine what is the best course for handling Joab—just make sure the result is that he's dead, not retired and living as a peaceful old man."

One of the great laws of the universe has always been "Live by the sword, die by the sword." Since David's early days with his gibborim, who had been his bloodiest soldier? Certainly it was Joab. He had killed ruthlessly and without remorse, not only in battle but in murderous feuds. Sometimes it was at David's command, such as with Uriah the Hittite. At other times he acted despite his king's commands, as he did with Abner, Absalom, and Amasa. Now it was Joab's turn in the circle of life to be the one who died by the sword.

It is strange for Joab, who had served David for so long, to wind up number one on the execution list. Was there no mercy for David's own nephew?

Joab himself made it clear that he was a dire threat to Solomon's kingdom. Joab had tipped his hand. His alliance with Adonijah was his death warrant. David knew that if at any point during Solomon's reign another opportunity presented itself for Joab to help someone else take the throne away by mutiny, the general would do so in the blink of an eye. Joab had to go.

Learning of the hit put out on him, Joab seeks sanctuary in the tabernacle. He grabs hold of the horns of the altar. Not wanting to shed blood inside God's tabernacle, Solomon sends his father's former advisor Benaiah in after Joab and demands that he come outside.

"No way!" Joab tells Benaiah. "I'm not leaving this place. I'll die here an old man if I have to. If the king wants me dead, he's just going to have to kill me right here."

Surely Joab assumed the tender young King Solomon would lack the nerve to kill anyone, especially a relative on the horns of the altar. Maybe he thought he could get Adonijah's deal and take early retirement in Galilee.

Benaiah returns to Solomon and explains the situation. "I wasn't so sure about taking a person's life right there on the altar, inside the tabernacle, with priests around watching, but he told me to tell you that if you want him dead, you're going to have to do it right there."

Without hesitation, Solomon replies, "Do as Joab said. You kill him right there on that altar. Long ago he thought he had to lure the pardoned Abner out of refuge in order to kill him, and he believes I feel the same constraint. I don't. Gut him where he is."

In what must have been a surprise for everyone, especially the refuge-seeking Joab, Benaiah walks right into the tabernacle and plunges his sword into the general. For over forty years Joab had lived by the sword. In a matter of seconds he died by it as well.

SHIMEI

"You are a wise man, and you will know how to arrange a bloody death for him" (1 Kings 2:9)—David's words to Solomon regarding the man who had cursed him and thrown rocks at him as he fled Jerusalem to escape from Absalom. This is shocking to us. Such an old wound. Such a petty insult. Remembered all those years? Enough to deserve death?

However, this scene was not merely a father and son sharing a final moment together. David and Solomon were kings in the early Iron Age, kings who were desperately trying to hold together a newborn kingdom by their fingernails. Previously, two civil wars had been fought to stave off rebellions, and a coup d'état was barely foiled when Solomon was hurriedly announced as David's successor. The dying king's reasons for commanding "a bloody death" for a curmudgeon are twofold. One, Solomon had to make it clear what will happen to instigators of internal uprisings and rebellions against the king. Two, public humiliations against the person of the king cannot go unpunished forever.

David told Solomon, "I swore to the Lord that I would never kill Shimei, but nothing was ever promised concerning you. As soon as I'm dead and buried, you take him out for me. When I needed support, all he had for me were curses and rocks. Don't be gentle on him, son."

In fact, Solomon does go easy on Shimei. He does not even exile him from Jerusalem. He does the exact opposite. He puts Shimei under house arrest.

"My father wanted you dead, but that's not what I'm going to do. Instead, build yourself a house here in Jerusalem and stay put. Never leave. If ever you so much as cross the Kidron Valley,

I will have you killed immediately. This is your second chance; there will not be a third."

Shimei eagerly agrees, though of course he had no other choice, and makes his permanent home in Jerusalem. Three years later, two of Shimei's slaves escaped to Gath, and he goes after them to bring them back to Jerusalem. Upon returning home, Shimei is sent for by one of the king's messengers.

"Didn't I tell you to never leave, to never cross the Kidron Valley?" the dismayed Solomon asks the foolish Shimei.

"Well, yeah, but I came right back, Your Majesty," Shimei tries explaining to him. "I didn't think you meant I literally couldn't ever cross the Kidron. I just needed to retrieve my escaped slaves and then I came right back."

"No, I meant literally. A king means exactly what he says. I tried to save your pathetic life." The king then turns to Benaiah, whom he had appointed to Joab's old position, and says, "Kill him."

ADONIJAH

David did not give orders concerning Adonijah when he issued his hit list. Even at the end, he could not come to terms with killing or even appropriately punishing one of his own children. He had refused to do so with Amnon and Absalom, and it is not surprising that he did not order Solomon to give Adonijah what he deserved. Adonijah would learn quickly enough that Solomon was not easily manipulated.

Shortly after David's death, Adonijah pays a visit to Bathsheba—the mother of the new king. There is no doubt that had Adonijah's coup succeeded, he would have killed Bathsheba. Adonijah is certainly the last person Bathsheba thought would ever ask her for a favor.

"Have you come to make trouble?" she rightfully asks her son's half brother, who had been told to behave forever or face death immediately.

"No, no, just the opposite. I've come for love," the wily politician assures her. "I have fallen in love with a girl, and I want to marry her. As you know, I tried to be king but that was not God's plan. I'm OK with that now. Really I am. Solomon is a wonderful king. Thankfully, I have discovered that happiness for me is not in sitting on the throne but in a girl, for I have fallen in love with Abishag, the young lady from Shunem. Would you please ask your son the king if I could marry her?" Abishag was the girl who had been David's bed warmer until his death.

Poor Bathsheba. Ever the romantic, was she not? While married to Uriah the Hittite, the king came calling and she was swept off her feet by his power, his royalty, and his romance. Because of romance, she had suffered misery and shame— forever the woman everyone pointed at behind her back.

Years later she still has not changed. The man who tried stealing the throne, a man whom she admitted with her own words would have had her killed as his first act as king, comes to her on behalf of "love," and her heart melts.

"Yes, I will go to my son on your behalf, Adonijah, and ask him to let you marry the love of your life."

The moment comes. What a scene it must have been.

"Mother?" Solomon says in disbelief. "Are you kidding me? What are you thinking? Why don't you just take the crown off my head right now and place it on Adonijah? Then we'll invite him over, give him the throne, and you and I can go take a short walk off a cliff together. That would be a whole lot easier and less painful than what would happen if we let the son of a king marry a girl with such an intimate relationship with the former king. The day after the wedding Adonijah and his friends would reunite for another dinner party and plan their next coup."

At this, Solomon sends for Adonijah and says, "I showed you mercy when I should've killed you. I won't make that mistake again, brother. I told you when last we spoke, complete loyalty or death."

He then turned to Benaiah and says to him, "Kill this fool."

Leadership Focus: It is not too late to affirm those who need encouragement from you.

> *As has been said already, David failed miserably when it came to family. He led Israel with wisdom, boldness, and the perfect blend of compassion and discipline. His leadership in the home was an entirely different story. His children were either at complete odds with him, to the point of trying to kill him, or they were barely mentioned in Scripture, as though they were not a focal point of the king's life.*
>
> *Here at the end of his life, in his final instructions to his son the king, David finally attempted to handle both Israel and family. He began his final conversation with his son by telling him: "I am going where everyone on earth must someday go. Take courage and be a man. Observe the requirements of the LORD your God, and follow all his ways. Keep the decrees, commands, regulations, and laws written in the Law of Moses so that you will be successful in all you do and wherever you go" (1 Kings 2:2–3).*

I wonder how long Solomon had waited to hear such words from his father. The son of Bathsheba had known only the life of royalty to which he was born. He had only known a kingdom full of war, internal strife, political conspiracy, and terrible family tensions. Solomon heard the whispers about his adulterous mother and saw the crowds gathered in support of his "more legitimate" brothers who also aspired to be king. All his life, the future builder of the temple probably longed for words of love, support, and wisdom from the greatest man he ever knew, but barely knew—his father.

Who in your life needs to hear and receive your support, your words of wisdom, and your love for them? Who needs to hear from their father, their pastor, their boss, or their mentor, "Take courage. Be a man. Follow God's ways"? Who needs your wise instructions on the first steps they should take in their new marriage, job, or responsibilities?

Most likely your advice would not be a list of those whom they should kill. I certainly hope not! The point is David was concerned with his son achieving the greatest success possible

When you are a leader, it means you have followers who are hoping to be leaders themselves. It is never too soon to start pouring into their lives and leadership. Do it now, while you are actively leading them. Don't wait until you are on your deathbed as David did.

EPILOGUE

God said, "I have found David son of
Jesse, a man after my own heart."
—Acts 13:22

THE QUESTION, THE real question about David still remains to be answered. Simply put, it is this: Why, how, can he possibly be called a man after God's own heart?

Imagine a jury sitting through a detailed recap of David's life—his sins, his struggles, his victories, his poems—and then being asked to deliberate until they can unanimously answer the question: "Was David truly a man after God's own heart?"

Consider again some of the highlights of the life of David.

- He killed and then posthumously circumcised two hundred Philistines for a bride price.

- He lied to a priest in order to eat holy bread, which led to the massacre of eighty-five priests and their families.

- He feigned madness in Gath after realizing his mistake in seeking refuge there.

- He slaughtered countless Amalekites, including women and children, in order to remain a top mercenary commander for the Philistines, who were enemies of Israel.

- He had the ark of the covenant carried into Jerusalem on an ox cart instead of by priests per God's command, which led to the death of a well-intentioned Israelite.

- He had an affair with Bathsheba, impregnated her, murdered her husband, and tried covering the whole thing up.

- He failed to discipline his son Amnon after Tamar's rape.

- He allowed Absalom to live without punishment, even after the prince murdered his brother.

- On his deathbed he instructed Solomon to kill a man because years earlier he had disrespected David.

All this, and God still called David "a man after My own heart"? How can that be right? Even for a Bronze Age warrior, some of these highlights of David's life are tough to read and still acknowledge the spiritual greatness of Israel's second king.

A Man After God's Own Heart

Shortly after David's last victory over the Philistines, the king decided that he wanted a census taken of all Israel—from Beersheba in the south to Dan in the north. He ordered Joab to total these numbers for him "so I may know how many people there are" (2 Sam. 24:2).

The prideful David wanted to revel in this number. He thought, "I want to know over how many I rule. I want to know how large my armies are. I want to know what the exact numbers are. I deserve to celebrate all I've accomplished as king."

In a surprising display of insight and fear of God, Joab, of all people, asked David not to do this. God had forbidden such a census for Israel, and the general, who was normally loyal to David beyond question and hardly ever squeamish about anything, did not want David and Israel to sin in this way or go through the punishment it would bring upon the nation. "But why, my lord the king, do you want to do this?...Why must you cause Israel to sin?" Joab asked his king (1 Chron. 21:3).

Despite Joab's warning and the reminder that God had forbidden Israel from numbering itself and basking in self-glory, David insisted on going forward. Joab reluctantly did what he was told.

To no one's surprise, God was displeased with the decision to take a census and sent Gad, David's spiritual advisor, to rebuke David. David, who had proven multiple times that he knew when to confess and how to repent, repented once again and called out to God. "I have sinned greatly by taking this census. Please forgive my guilt for doing this foolish thing" (1 Chron. 21:8).

Was David forgiven? Did God remove his sin "as far away from [David] as the east is from the west," as David wrote in Psalm 103:12? Of course. Our God is gracious and quick to forgive, but God's forgiveness does not always stop the destruction. Sin can be forgiven. Sin also has consequences, and David's most destructive sin was not sexual lust, as many think. It was pride.

David had knowingly disobeyed God, despite being warned by Joab, and though he repented, discipline came—harsh discipline. Gad told David that God would allow him to choose Israel's punishment: "These are the choices the LORD has given you. You may choose three years of famine, three months of destruction by the sword of your enemies, or three days of severe plague as the angel of the LORD brings devastation throughout the land of Israel" (1 Chron. 21:11–12).

In short, God told David, "You counted all those people and you wanted to take pride in it; I will now diminish that number.

Your vanity in the number over whom you rule will be the cause of deaths in the tens of thousands."

Upon hearing the punishment choices from Gad, David was horrified, of course, but he knew God's grace, even in terrible judgment, was his only chance. He told Gad, "I don't ever wish to fall into the hands of our enemy. Even now, even in judgment, I believe in the mercies of God. I choose the plague from the angel of the Lord."

Over the next three days, a deadly plague devastated Israel. Seventy thousand people died. On the third day, God sent a destroying angel with a sword stretched out against Jerusalem. Just as the angel was ready to strike a crushing blow to the capital city the merciful God whom David trusted cried out to the angel, "Stop! That is enough!" (1 Chron. 21:15)

In that moment, David and the leaders with him fell on their faces and David called out to God, "It's me who sinned. I'm the one who called for the census, not any of these people. Take out your anger on me, not on those innocent of this crime. I plead with you, O Lord! Take my life, no one else's!"

At that God spoke to David, "There is a massive stone nearby owned by a Jebusite named Araunah who uses it as a threshing floor. I want you to go buy that spot from him and build Me an altar on that rock and offer Me a sacrifice from that very altar."

David quickly arose and ran to Araunah's threshing floor. The angel of the Lord, sword still in hand, stood behind David where Araunah and his four sons could see him. The king told the land owner, "I need to buy this threshing floor and the rock it sits on. I will build an altar to the Lord on it and bring an end to this plague!"

The very sight of the terrifying angel was enough to convince Araunah, who cried out, "Just take it. It's yours! Use my oxen for the burnt offering and my wheat for the grain offering. Whatever you need!"

David would not accept the gracious offer. "I cannot offer a sacrifice to God that didn't cost me anything," David told him. "I must pay full price. Don't even cut me a deal."

As soon as the purchase was consummated, David built an altar and sacrificed burnt offerings and peace offerings to the Lord. As David prayed, the Lord sent fire down from heaven to burn up, or accept, the offering and commanded the angel to put away his sword. Jerusalem was spared.

When David saw that God had shown mercy to Jerusalem and that the plague was over, he offered another sacrifice on the newly built altar. Then he made a proclamation that has impacted history for three thousand years. "This will now be the permanent place of the altar for Israel's burnt offerings. This will be where God's temple will stand!"

That great stone represented perhaps David's most grievous sin, which was vainglory, a sin that caused a hideous plague that killed seventy thousand people in Israel. That stone also became a place of worship and repentance and restoration. Through it all—dodging spears from his father-in law, hiding in caves, pretending to be loyal to Gath, losing Ziklag, a wife who despised him, sons who tried to dethrone him, lifelong allies who betrayed him, innocent baby taken from him, famine, rebellions, political conspiracies, and plagues—David loved and trusted God.

David was not perfect. Far from it. His sins were real. His repentance was also real as was his faith in the mercy of God.

I trust in your unfailing love. I will rejoice because you have rescued me. I will sing to the LORD because he has been so good to me.

—DAVID THE GREAT, PSALM 13:5–6

Still the question haunts. A man after God's heart? Really?

Perhaps the best answer is found in a mysterious moment before David even appears on the stage. Samuel was sent to Bethlehem by God, there to anoint Saul's successor.

Directed to Jesse's house, Samuel looked over the sons whom Jesse presented. Starting with the eldest and working his way down the line of ever-so-sturdy farm boys, Samuel studied the lineup. He was impressed. These were champions, milk-fed militiamen whose strong arms could wield a sword or a scythe with equal effect.

God's answer, however, was, "It is none of these." It was not, however, that none of them measured up. It was rather that there was no physical measurement with which Samuel might size up the winner. God wanted the prophet to understand God's view is not ours.

But the LORD said unto Samuel, Look not on his countenance, or on the height of his stature; because I have refused [the eldest son of Jesse]; for the LORD seeth not as man seeth; for man looketh on the outward appearance, but the LORD looketh on the heart.

—1 SAMUEL 16:7, KJV

Therein lies the answer to David: his heart in the eyes of God. God saw something in David's heart that God loved and never gave up on. Somehow, out there all alone in the wilderness with his sheep, young David found favor in the eyes of God. What shall we call it? Faith? Love? Perhaps it defies our Western obsession with analytics.

The relationship between David and God was a like a long and stormy marriage. They loved, struggled, made up, started over, and struggled again, but they never gave up on each other.

Why David and not Saul? Saul sinned wretchedly, but then so did David. Saul's heart, his innermost self was bent away from God. The sinful ellipse of Saul's life never circled back to God. It just kept going, looping further and further away until it ended in madness and witchcraft and suicide.

Unlike Saul, the trajectory of David's whole life was God-ward. Even in sin and failure, that God-ward momentum always kept David from the abyss. David trusted God. David never didn't believe in God. David never gave up on God, and he believed that God would never give up on him.

We who are so quick to judge each other are also delighted to judge the likes of David. God's favor on David's life disturbs us. It upsets our theological and legalistic apple carts. It sorely tempts us to argue with God, to whine about the divine fascination with this not-so-holy Jewish king.

"Look at him, Lord," we want to complain. "Look at what he did. Look how he sinned. It's right there in the Bible. Look at his life. What did you see in him?"

"That's just it," answers the Lord, "I saw *in* him. You can see David's sins. So did I, and he suffered for them. You see his life from the outside. I saw in him. I saw the heart of My servant David, and I knew that his heart was after My heart. I never forgot that. Sometimes David forgot, but I never did."

Surely goodness and mercy shall follow me all the days of my life, and I will dwell in the house of the LORD forever.

—DAVID THE GREAT, PSALM 23:6, NKJV

NOTES

INTRODUCTION

1. Isaiah Gafni, "Herod the Great," My Jewish Learning, accessed October 10, 2017, https://www.myjewishlearning.com/article/herod-the-great/.

CHAPTER 3
THE NEW HEBREW IDOL

1. C. S. Lewis, *The Four Loves* (New York: Harcourt, 1960), 87–104.

CHAPTER 4
FROM HERO TO MADMAN

1. Blue Letter Bible, s.v. *"gibbowr,"* accessed October 10, 2017, https://www.blueletterbible.org/lang/lexicon/lexicon.cfm?Strongs=H1368&t=KJV.

CHAPTER 5
FROM MADMAN TO MERCENARY

1. "En Gedi," BiblePlaces.com, accessed October 10, 2017, https://www.bibleplaces.com/engedi/.

CHAPTER 7
WIVES, LIVES, AND COLLATERAL DAMAGE

1. Blue Letter Bible, s.v. *"Nabal,"* accessed October 11, 2017, https://www.blueletterbible.org/lang/lexicon/lexicon.cfm?Strongs=H5037&t=KJV.
2. "When Elephants Fight, It Is the Grass That Suffers Most," *Africa Geographic*, March 3, 2017, https://africageographic.com/blog/elephants-fight-grass-suffers/.

CHAPTER 10
THE GIRL WITH THE CURL

1.   Henry Wadsworth Longfellow, "There Was a Little Girl," Bartleby.com, accessed October 12, 2017, http://www.bartleby.com /360/1/120.html.

2.   Johann Wolfgang von Goethe, *Faust, Part One* (New York: Dover Publications, 1994), 13, https://books.google.com/books?id =gjfDAgAAQBAJ&pg.

CHAPTER 11
YOU ARE THE MAN

1.   Alfred Jones, *Jones' Dictionary of Old Testament Proper Names,* s.v. "Jedidiah" (Grand Rapids, MI: Kregel Publications, 1997), https://www.amazon.com/Jones-Dictionary-Testament-Proper-Names /dp/0825429617.

LEADERSHIP TRAINING THAT WILL CHANGE YOUR LIFE FOREVER.

Dr. Mark Rutland believes in transformational change. With a history of successfully turning organizations around, he knows that leadership training isn't a thing you do just once - it is a process. That is why he has developed the National Institute of Christian Leadership, a program designed to help you take your church, ministry or business to the next level.

The National Institute of Christian Leadership lets you interact with Dr. Rutland up close and personal and then process and apply what you have learned to your own situation. You get graduate-level leadership training that is intense, personal, practical and relevant.

For more information,
please visit

thenicl.com

Sessions Include
- Change Dynamics
- Strategic Growth
- Transformational Management
- Communication and Worship

NICL
NATIONAL INSTITUTE OF CHRISTIAN LEADERSHIP